Guiding

Young People

in Bible Study

W. L. HOWSE

CONVENTION PRESS

Nashville, Tennessee

Code Number: Church Study Course

This book is number 1751 in category 17, section for
Adults and Young People.

Library of Congress Catalog Card Number: 55-14855
Printed in the United States of America
5.AT 63 R.R.D.

To Bill

Who Is My Best Teacher and Pupil

About the Author

WILLIAM LEWIS HOWSE, JR., is a native Tennessean, born at Fayetteville. He received the A.B. and LL.D. degrees from Union University, the M.A. degree from Baylor University, and the M.R.E. and D.R.E. degrees from Southwestern Baptist Theological Seminary. He holds the L.H.D. degree from Hardin-Simmons University.

Dr. Howse served as minister of education of the Broadway Baptist Church, Fort Worth (1927-30 and 1935-45); Seventh and James Street Baptist Church, Waco (1930-32); Polytechnic Baptist Church, Fort Worth (1933-35); First Baptist Church, Dallas (1946); and University Baptist Church, Fort Worth (1947-49). He was professor in the School of Religious Education at the Southwestern Baptist Theological Seminary (1932-54).

Dr. Howse served as president of Texas Baptist Training Union Convention (1929-32), Texas Baptist Training Union Executive Board (1935-37), Southwestern Baptist Religious Education Association (1941), and Texas Baptist Sunday School Convention (1946-51).

At the invitation of the Foreign Mission Board in 1952, Dr. Howse toured the mission fields of South America in the interest of religious education. A more extensive tour was made in 1956, including Hawaii, the Orient, Southeast Asia, and Australia. In 1957, by invitation of the Home Mission Board, Dr. Howse visited the mission fields of Cuba. In 1958 he made a trip around the world, leading conferences on Bible teaching and membership training.

Other books by Dr. Howse are *Teaching Young People in the Sunday School, In Spirit and in Truth, The Sunday School and Missions, The Church Staff and Its Work,* and *Those Treasured Hours.*

Since 1954 Dr. Howse has served as director of the Education Division of the Baptist Sunday School Board.

Dr. and Mrs. Howse have one son, William Lewis III.

Contents

Church Study Course

THE CHURCH STUDY COURSE began October 1, 1959. It is a merger of three courses previously promoted by the Sunday School Board—the Sunday School Training Course, the Graded Training Union Study Course, and the Church Music Training Course. On October 1, 1961, the Woman's Missionary Union principles and methods studies were added.

The course is fully graded. The system of awards provides a series of five diplomas of twenty books each for Adults or Young People, two diplomas of five books each for Intermediates, and two diplomas of five books each for Juniors. Book awards earned previously in the Sunday School Training Course, the Graded Training Union Study Course, and the Church Music Training Course may be transferred to the new course.

The course is comprehensive, with books grouped into twenty categories. The purpose of the course is to help Christians to grow in knowledge and conviction, to help them to grow toward maturity in Christian character and competence for service, to encourage them to participate worthily as workers in their churches, and to develop leaders for all phases of church life and work.

The Church Study Course is promoted by the Baptist Sunday School Board, 127 Ninth Avenue, North, Nashville, Tennessee 37203, through its Sunday School, Training Union, Church Music, and Church Administration departments; by the Woman's Missionary Union, 600 North Twentieth Street, Birmingham, Alabama 35203; and by the respective departments in the states affiliated with the Southern Baptist Convention. A description of the course and the system of awards may be found in the leaflet, "Trained Workmen," which may be obtained without charge from any one of these departments.

A record of all awards earned should be maintained in each church. A person should be designated by the church to keep the files. Forms for such records may be ordered from any Baptist Book Store.

Requirements for Credit in Class or Home Study

IF CREDIT is desired for the study of this book in a class or by home study, the following requirements must be met:

I. IN CLASSWORK

1. The class must meet a minimum of seven and one-half clock hours. The required time does not include assembly periods. Ten class periods of forty-five minutes each are recommended. (If laboratory or clinical work is desired in specialized or technical courses, this requirement may be met by six clock hours of classwork and three clock hours of supervised laboratory or clinical work.)

2. A class member who attends all class sessions and completes the reading of the book within a week following the last class session will not be required to do any written work for credit.

3. A class member who is absent from one or more sessions must answer the questions (pp. 149–150) on all chapters he misses. In such a case, he must turn in his paper within a week, and he must certify that he has read the book.

4. The teacher should request an award for himself. A person who teaches a book in the section for Intermediates or Juniors (any category) or conducts an approved unit of instruction for Nursery, Beginner, or Primary children will be granted an award in category 11, Special Studies, which will count as an elective on his own diploma. He should specify in his request the name of the book taught, or the unit conducted for Nursery, Beginner, or Primary children.

5. The teacher should complete the "Request for Book Awards—Class Study" (Form 150) and forward it within two weeks after the completion of the class to the Church Study Course Awards Office, 127 Ninth Avenue, North, Nashville Tennessee 37203.

II. In Home Study

1. A person who does not attend any class session may receive credit by answering all questions for written work as indicated in the book (pp. 149–150). When a person turns in his paper on home study, he must certify that he has read the book.

2. Students may find profit in studying the text together, but individual papers are required. Carbon copies or duplicates in any form cannot be accepted.

3. Home study work papers may be graded by the pastor or a person designated by him, or they may be sent to the Church Study Course Awards Office for grading. The form entitled "Request for Book Awards—Home Study" (Form 151) must be used in requesting awards. It should be mailed to Church Study Course Awards Office, 127 Ninth Avenue, North, Nashville, Tennessee 37203.

III. Credit for This Book

This book is number 1751 in category 17, section for Adults and Young People.

GUIDING YOUNG PEOPLE
IN BIBLE STUDY

CHAPTER 1

I. THE PLACE OF THE TEACHER IN THE YOUNG PEOPLE'S CLASS

   1. A Position of Honor and Trust
   2. An Interpreter of Truth
   3. A Guide in Learning

II. SOME QUALIFICATIONS OF THE YOUNG PEOPLE'S TEACHER

   1. A Redeemed Soul
   2. A Responsive Mind
   3. A Consecrated Body
   4. Dedicated Talents
   5. A Will to Succeed
   6. A Desire to Work
   7. An Enthusiasm for the Task

III. SOME UNDESIRABLE TRAITS OF THE YOUNG PEOPLE'S TEACHER

   1. Self-centered and Selfish
   2. Love for Power
   3. Too Meticulous
   4. Satisfaction with Previous Attainments
   5. Influenced by Moods

IV. GREAT TEACHERS MAKE THEIR PUPILS GREAT

   1. Lessons and Teachers
   2. The Importance of the Teacher

1

The Teacher of Young People

Take heed unto thyself (1 Tim. 4:16)

THE TERM "teacher" was used often in connection with the earthly ministry of Christ. When he finished teaching on the mountain, they said of him, "He taught them as one having authority, and not as the scribes" (Matt. 7:29). Nicodemus said to him, "We know that thou art a teacher come from God" (John 3:2). One who teaches today follows in the glorious tradition of the master Teacher.

I. THE PLACE OF THE TEACHER IN THE YOUNG PEOPLE'S CLASS

The teacher occupies the most important office in the class. His opportunities for service are unlimited because of the very nature of this office.

1. *A Position of Honor and Trust*

It is indeed an honor to be asked to teach young people. This period of life, which includes young men and young women seventeen to twenty-four years of age, is one of the most significant of the entire life span. The invitation in itself implies that the church believes in the prospective teacher's spiritual fitness to teach this age group. It recognizes in him talents and abilities for teaching which he himself may not have recognized. The church believes in his capacity for growth. It believes he has something to share with young people.

But his selection does not imply in any way that being a teacher is an "honorary" position. A church does not seek to put certain members in positions simply to honor them. Teaching is a place of sacred trust and service. The teacher is selected to exert a positive Christian influence. He becomes a "marked" personality in the church and community. He must live a better-than-average Christian life and prove by his faith and service the depth of his Christian experience. There are things he must not do, places he must not frequent, and conversation in which he must not indulge, if he meets the requirements of his office.

2. *An Interpreter of Truth*

Young people are seekers after truth, and those who teach them have the privilege of interpreting ageless truth to them. The Bible was written for every generation. Its message is not out of date nor shall it ever be. The teacher who can say with Paul, "I know" and who can interpret clearly "Thus saith the Lord" will take his place in the confidence of his class membership.

The successful teacher of young people has the privilege of interpreting Bible truth in relation to the experiences which young people are having. It is only when truth is interpreted in relation to life that it becomes significant. The teacher's task is to do this so attractively that young people will desire to appropriate the truth for themselves.

3. *A Guide in Learning*

The task of the teacher is to stimulate learning. Horace Mann indicated that a teacher who was trying to teach without inspiring his pupils to learn was hammering on cold iron. A teacher should not be pointing to the path of knowledge and learning, but should be actively leading his class along that path.

It is not enough to know a lesson. The teacher must know it in such a way as to inspire and stimulate his pupils to learn it.

II. SOME QUALIFICATIONS OF THE YOUNG PEOPLE'S TEACHER

If the office brings something of significance to the teacher, then the teacher should bring something worth while to the office. What the teacher is, is more important than what he says or what he does. But all these things are important in the teaching process.

The responsibilities connected with the teacher's work are so great that almost everyone will shrink from accepting them. This is especially true as one studies a list of qualifications for teaching. However, this discussion is intended as a set of goals for the teacher who aspires to improve himself in the art of teaching.

One just beginning to teach was impressed by the knowledge and skill of another who had devoted a quarter of a century to this ministry. After observing his abilities, he said timidly, "I would give almost anything to be able to teach like you." To this the skilful teacher replied, "If you will devote yourself to it for twenty-five years you can." What then are some desirable qualities for those who teach young people?

1. *A Redeemed Soul*

Anyone who is to teach the Christian way of life must himself be a Christian. This involves more than just an affirmation. A Christian is one who has accepted Christ as his personal Saviour and as a result of this experience has become a loyal follower of Christ. In following Christ he has been baptized into the fellowship of a church and is actively engaged in its work.

Personal experience is the basic qualification of everyone who is to teach others about Christ. One cannot teach what he does not know. What he knows with assurance will find its way into his teaching.

A story is told of an elderly minister and an actor who were in a small circle of friends. The actor was asked to quote the twenty-third Psalm and he did it so perfectly the group applauded him. Then they turned to the elderly minister and asked him to quote it. Having used it on many occasions to bring comfort to bereaved ones, he quoted it with all the meaning which the psalm had for him. When he finished, his friends were in tears. The actor was among the first to speak. "I know the psalm," said he, "but you know the Shepherd of the psalm." In teaching Bible truth this is the most important knowledge for the teacher to possess.

2. *A Responsive Mind*

Anyone who succeeds with young people must be mentally alert. He is dealing with growing youth at the peak of their intellectual vigor. This should not frighten him, but compel him to make adequate preparation. No teacher can be prepared to answer all the questions his pupils will ask him. But the very fact that these questions are asked will inspire the teacher to be alert and studious. If he does not know the answers to their questions, he has the best possible stimulus for additional study.

It is such study which will ultimately lead to self-confidence in teaching. To know that one knows a thing gives assurance which nothing else can give. Scholarship is the answer to the sense of insecurity in teaching. Jesus' example in this realm will prove inspiring to those who teach today. Matthew gives this record of his teaching in Nazareth: "And when he was come into his own country, he taught them in their synagogue, insomuch that they were astonished, and said, Whence hath this

man this wisdom, and these mighty works?" (Matt. 13:
54). John gives this account of the reactions of some of his
hearers: "And the Jews marvelled, saying, How knoweth
this man letters, having never learned?" (John 7:15).
The answer Jesus gave to their statement is revealing:
"My doctrine is not mine, but his that sent me" (John
7:16).

Although no one can teach as Jesus taught, all have access to this same source of power which he had and are
urged to avail themselves of it: "If any of you lack wisdom, let him ask of God, that giveth to all men liberally,
and upbraideth not; and it shall be given him. But let
him ask in faith, nothing wavering" (James 1:5-6).

The teacher's ability to reason and think appeals to
young people. Willingness to listen to their point of view
and discuss various angles of a difficult subject wins confidence as few things will. One reason why many young
people drop out of Sunday school is because they are not
challenged to think.

3. A Consecrated Body

Anyone responsible for the spiritual guidance of others
must give attention to the use of his physical body. It is
the agent of the service he renders. He should conserve
and utilize its energies. He should not cripple his usefulness through what he takes into his body nor by what he
does with it. "Daniel purposed in his heart that he would
not defile himself with the portion of the king's meat,
nor with the wine which he drank" (Dan. 1:8). If every
teacher would be equally conscientious in facing his
temptations, a victory for righteousness would result.

It will be impossible for the teacher to keep secret
what he does. If there is a conflict between what he says
and what his conduct reveals, his influence for good will
be lost upon those whom he seeks to teach.

Paul wrote to the Corinthians, "What? know ye not that your body is the temple of the Holy Ghost which is in you, which ye have of God, and ye are not your own? For ye are bought with a price: therefore glorify God in your body, and in your spirit, which are God's (1 Cor. 6:19-20).

To the Romans he wrote, "I beseech you therefore, brethren, by the mercies of God, that ye present your bodies a living sacrifice, holy, acceptable unto God, which is your reasonable service" (Rom. 12:1).

It was evident to Paul that the use to which one put his body had profound influence upon the quality of his service for Christ.

4. Dedicated Talents

It is a great asset for one to have many talents and abilities. But if these are not dedicated to Christ, they will prove of little value in the ministry of Sunday school teaching. The teacher must place all the talents he possesses at the disposal of the Holy Spirit.

There is danger in self-confidence and assurance. If one feels fully qualified to teach, this is one of the most conclusive indications that he is not qualified. Christ said, "I am the vine, ye are the branches: He that abideth in me, and I in him, the same bringeth forth much fruit: for without me ye can do nothing" (John 15:5). It is not alone the abilities of the teacher which make for success in teaching. It is his ability to let them become the channel of God's grace which will cause him to succeed.

It is the willingness to become an instrument in the hand of God which gives power and influence to the talents one possesses. A highly educated woman remonstrated with D. L. Moody because of his use of poor grammar in one of his messages. To this, Mr. Moody is said to have replied, "I am using all the grammar I know for the glory of God."

If God could transform a rod in the hand of Moses into a serpent and could use the lunch of one boy to feed a multitude, he can take the talents of even a mediocre person and use them to accomplish great things.

5. A Will to Succeed

Halfhearted, slip-shod efforts have no place in the program of Christ. Every teacher should desire to succeed at his task. Young people are quick to recognize success in any realm. Thus, those who are successful as housewives, teachers, farmers, lawyers, businessmen and women, or at whatever task they may be doing, will have greater influence.

But success in one's vocation does not guarantee success in the field of Sunday school teaching. To succeed in this field one must know pupil life, the Bible, the work of his church and denomination, how people learn, how to teach, and many other fields of study.

To have a passive desire often expressed in the statement, "I wish I were better prepared," is not enough. Wishing, by itself, never made any person better. One needs to put action to his wishes.

6. A Desire to Work

Sunday school work is work. The word "work" should never be emphasized lightly. Work determines the type of worker one becomes. Work determines the quality of Sunday school teaching, the size of the class, the number of new converts, and the general progress from year to year.

Not all workers are workers. Some who bear the name do nothing between Sundays other than make a token preparation for teaching. Greeted only by the faithful few on Sunday, they wonder what is the matter. Lack of work is the answer. Work transforms the worker as well as the task.

Some work spasmodically and become discouraged when they do not achieve all the results they expected. Others work when they feel like it and that is distressingly infrequent.

Every worker, working every week will build a Sunday school anywhere. The need is not for more and better schemes for building classes but better workers working harder every week according to plans which have been tested and found effective.

By work is meant preparation for teaching, attending the weekly officers and teachers' meeting, personal visitation, and conducting class business meetings, all of which are responsibilities of the teacher.

A denominational worker visiting a business institution asked the elevator operator how many people worked there. The operator thought for a moment and replied, "Oh, about half of 'em, I guess." Is that true where you work?

The teacher should work not for the approval of the pastor or superintendent, although each should be observant and quick to express his appreciation for work well done. But a teacher's work is subject to God's approval. Paul had something of this in mind when he wrote to Timothy, "Study to shew thyself approved unto God, a workman that needeth not to be ashamed, rightly dividing the word of truth" (2 Tim. 2:15).

7. An Enthusiasm for the Task

The enthusiasm of youth responds to the enthusiasm of the teacher. This does not mean that every session of the class should resemble a pep rally. It need not be noisy, carefree, nor devoted primarily to handshaking and fellowship. Certainly friendliness and good will should prevail, and a hearty welcome should be given to all.

But a teacher sensing the challenge, seeing the possibilities in the task, and devoting himself to his work will have a contagious enthusiasm which members of the class will recognize.

There is much in American life to appeal to the enthusiasm of youth. Unless there is some enthusiasm in the Sunday school class, young people will not be attracted to it.

A later discussion will deal with the physical aspects of this subject. But it should be stated here, a teacher must be at his best physically if he is to lead young people. Many times a tired body will defeat a well-prepared mind.

Spirit makes the difference in a business, a team, an institution, and a person. A pessimistic teacher is out of place in a Young People's class. Either he should change his attitude or his position. It is not the place for anyone who carries a grudge. A recent newspaper statement carries the thought in these words, "The person with a chip on his shoulder has more wood higher up."

God took note of Caleb's spirit when he said, "But my servant Caleb, because he had another spirit with him, and hath followed me fully, him will I bring into the land whereinto he went; and his seed shall possess it" (Num. 14:24).

III. Some Undesirable Traits of the Young People's Teacher

To be successful, one who teaches must not only cultivate positive qualities but must seek to avoid or eliminate negative traits. A few of these will be discussed briefly to indicate their nature and undesirability.

1. *Self-centered and Selfish*

The tendency is to notice this in others but to overlook it in oneself. Most persons are selfish and some are extremely so. We are commanded to love our neighbors as ourselves, but this few ever achieve. The simple truth is we love ourselves more than we love others. The words of a popular song of a few decades ago come to mind in this connection, "I love me, I love me, I'm wild about myself."

Often this hinders the usefulness of a teacher. Having the largest class, having taught for the longest period of time, meeting in the best room, and other things are often considered as badges of significance and importance. Many teachers have stood in the way of progress by refusing to start other classes or give up members. While other reasons are given, frequently the main reason may be traced to a selfish attitude.

2. *Love for Power*

Some teachers seemingly are never affected by the recognition and acclaim which they receive. But for some the slightest increase in responsibility becomes an incentive to control and dominate completely.

Any person who demands that he must be consulted about every decision, often absenting himself from regular meetings where such matters are discussed, is taking the energies of church leadership away from matters vastly more important in order to deal with his pettiness.

A teacher who dominates a class, who clashes with his department superintendent, general superintendent, or pastor, and who often tries to crush others in order to advance himself, should ask himself the question, "What is the matter with *me*?" He should read often, "Be kindly affectioned one to another with brotherly love; in honour preferring one another" (Rom. 12:10).

3. *Too Meticulous*

Some teachers may be bothered with the problem of being too exact about meaningless details. Everything must be done just one way and according to specifications. According to this formula, the success of the Sunday morning session is judged by the perfection with which it is conducted. The opposite attitude would be satisfaction with a haphazard procedure. The teacher of young people should take his position between these two extremes.

Simply carrying out the teacher's plans will be meaningless unless the reasons for doing so are understood by the class members. Perfection is not the goal. The goal is the development of young people so they may understand and achieve the fullest possible Christian growth.

4. *Satisfaction with Previous Attainments*

Often satisfaction is more deadly than failure. Failure may stimulate one to greater efforts, but satisfaction has the opposite effect. One who has taught his best lesson or developed his best class has reached the peak of his usefulness. No matter how many successes a teacher may have had, he should be looking ahead to others which are greater.

One of the best indications of satisfaction is the expression, "We used to have" or "I used to be." No Christian worker should be coasting on what happened in the past.

5. *Influenced by Moods*

This varies with the temperament of the person. Some are so moody as to disqualify themselves as teachers. But most individuals face this problem in varying degrees. Learning to work with one's moods is basic to success in leadership.

One business executive pointed out he made his plans for the future when he felt at his best. He laid these aside until he was somewhat despondent. Midway between elation and depression he found a plan which was acceptable. If he could not master his moods, at least he mastered the technique of working with them.

A teacher who is on the mountain peak one Sunday and in the valley the next will not have the balance necessary to guide growing life.

IV. Great Teachers Make Their Pupils Great

The most influential factor in the teaching process is the personality of the teacher.

1. *Lessons and Teachers*

Pupils forget lessons but remember teachers. After all, the best teachers teach life itself. If a teacher is a well-balanced personality, meeting the problems of life, adjusting wisely to them, and applying the teachings of Christ at all times to the best of his knowledge and ability, he will lead his pupils in attaining much of what he himself is experiencing. Real teaching occurs when pupils remember lessons because their teachers live them.

2. *The Importance of the Teacher*

More than methods, adequate space and equipment, and knowledge of the subject is the importance of the teacher himself. If he is great, great pupils are assured.

President James A. Garfield was so impressed by his college president, Mark Hopkins, that later he paid him a great tribute. He said if he had to make a choice between a well-equipped university with routine professors and Mark Hopkins in a tent, he would take the latter. Thus Mark Hopkins on one end of a log and a student on the other has become one of the most widely used illustrations to indicate the importance of the teacher in the learning process.

FOR FURTHER STUDY

1. Give four necessary qualifications of a teacher of young people. How would you rate yourself regarding these: below average, average, or above average?
2. Why is a teacher's enthusiasm so important?
3. Name three undesirable traits which teachers should avoid. Which one of these seems to be the greatest handicap? Why?
4. Do you believe "great teachers make their pupils great"? Give reasons for your answer.

CHAPTER 2

2

Understanding Teaching

*Teaching them to observe all things whatsoever
I have commanded you* (Matt. 28:20)

TEACHING is difficult to understand and define. It is safe
to say that no one understands fully the learning process.
The personalities of teachers and learners differ widely.
Their temperaments, intelligence, ambitions, and experiences are but a few of the areas in which there are
marked differences. What will stimulate one pupil to
learn will not influence another.

Teaching then can never become routine. There are
fundamental principles which underlie the processes of
teaching and learning, but these can never be standard-
ized into a set of foolproof rules.

Concepts of what is involved in the teaching process
vary with different teachers. Most young people's teachers are enlisted from Adult classes. As members of these
classes they are accustomed mainly to the lecture method
of teaching. Thus they think of lecturing as teaching. The
lecture is one of the methods of teaching, but it is only
one.

Other teachers, because of lack of understanding and
training may think of teaching as asking questions, reading from lesson helps, or simply letting young people talk
as they will during the lesson period.

I. SOME UNSATISFACTORY CONCEPTS OF TEACHING

Successful teaching begins with an understanding of
what teaching is. There are many false impressions about
it.

15

If teaching is to be effective, it must be understood. There are many ideas regarding teaching which are totally inadequate. Some of these ideas will be analyzed so that their inadequacies may be understood.

1. *Telling Others How to Live*

The idea that teaching is telling others how to live is somewhat prevalent. Those who hold to this concept believe that the teacher learns all he can about the lesson, then tells it to his members. It is assumed that the members listen, understand, and then try to apply what they have heard.

Certainly telling, or oral communication, is a part of all teaching, and the teacher must study and learn the truth of each lesson. But telling a person the truth of the lesson and what to do about it is not enough.

The pupil may not listen attentively while the teacher is talking. If he is listening, he may not correctly understand what he hears. If he hears correctly, he may be indifferent to it either because he feels it does not apply to him or because he is not interested.

If he is to learn the truth and apply it, he will need more to motivate him than the mere telling of the truth. One cannot pass over truth to another person as he would hand over money.

The teacher's task is to create an attitude of mind which will be conducive to acquiring knowledge and acting upon the truth which is learned.

2. *Bringing the Lesson to the Class*

One often hears the expression, "The teacher brought the lesson." Here the emphasis is on the lesson itself. The teacher "gets" the lesson by spending enough time in study to cover the Bible material and read the lesson helps. Too often, the teacher has only a general idea of the needs of the class. Instead he should have specific information regarding the needs of each member. With only general information as a guide, he strikes a common denominator and plans his lesson accordingly. A teacher who "brings a lesson" will do some good, but he will accomplish much more if he will enlarge the scope of his work.

Teaching is retail, not wholesale. The class as such does not learn. Individual members do the learning. Thus teaching becomes a particular rather than a general activity. The teacher must not think of teaching the class but of teaching its individual members.

3. Meeting with the Class on Sunday

Being faithful to one's responsibility and meeting with one's class each Sunday is a habit more teachers need to form. The absent teacher, be he ever so well prepared and capable, is a liability. But teaching is more than meeting with a class.

Some seem to feel their responsibility is discharged simply by being faithful. If little effort is put forth in study and learning, they do not seem discouraged in their efforts. Often, both teacher and class resort to superficial means to cover up the obvious lack of Bible study. Under this concept, teaching takes a back seat to be replaced by contests, an emphasis upon social life, and other things. Being with the class on Sunday is the goal of the teacher. The many fruitful learning activities of the weekdays are neglected. As a rule a class taught on this basis is without aim or purpose.

4. Taking Up the Time

Each teacher is confronted with the use of thirty minutes on Sunday. How to use this time most effectively is a problem for every teacher. Some feel that if they can plan the lesson so as to be through when the bell rings, they have done a creditable task. With a minimum knowledge of the Bible and teaching procedure, using the time at his disposal becomes quite a problem for the beginning teacher. It will be embarrassing if the teacher runs out of something to say ten minutes before the bell rings. So the goal of the teacher becomes that of synchronizing his lesson with the time limit.

This often rules out questions of vital interest to the pupil because the teacher does not have time for them. He must cover the lesson as planned. He does not welcome discussion, for that would eliminate some of the things he has planned to say. So his teaching revolves around the time at his disposal. This contributes to a passive class which must co-operate with a teacher whose principal goal is reaching a climax before the bell rings.

Teaching to take up time could mean just the opposite of this attitude. Then the teacher would welcome any question or discussion which would take up the time. If the members take part, it may delight the teacher even though conversation is far removed from the central truth of the lesson. He may feel he is accomplishing something by getting the members to participate. Participation is fine if there is some purpose or aim in it. But if the period of Bible study becomes a talk-fest, little actual learning will result.

Let us examine some ideas of teaching which will provide a more complete understanding of what is involved in the teaching-learning process.

II. Some More Adequate Concepts of Teaching

We have seen that teaching cannot be reduced to a patented formula. The teacher through a predetermined routine may lead his members to cover a series of Bible lessons for a quarter rather thoroughly. But after doing so, the teacher must be concerned in knowing what the pupils have received which will be of lasting value. Because many teachers do achieve results which contribute to the continuous spiritual growth of their members, teaching has been defined as an art.

1. *An Art*

Teaching is an art, for it deals with the guidance of growing personality. The painter works with pigments and canvas. The composer produces music from the harmony within himself. The sculptor brings a figure out of marble. The architect puts into sketches and blueprints the building which is to be.

But the teacher is more fortunate than any of these artists. He is dealing with the finest material of all, human personality. And the Sunday school teacher is not dealing solely with the human aspects of personality. He is concerned with the redemption of the person and his growth toward Christlikeness. This concept means that the work of the Sunday school teacher has significance in terms of eternity.

When the work of other artists has faded or crumbled, the artistry of the Sunday school teacher will still be at work in the world as his influence lives on in the lives of others.

As one considers a successful artist in any field, he is impressed with the preparation which is necessary. The artist must know how to handle the proper tools and materials. This comes by hours of study and experience. Any competent artist has spent years in the mastery of his craft. It has required unceasing labor and sacrifice. He has observed the work of others, but he has practiced constantly himself.

To anyone who has visited an art gallery it becomes apparent that each artist has followed the same basic principles in his work. But each has painted in his own way so there is something distinctive about the work of each.

When one has studied the craft of a particular artist for some time, he will be able to discern those certain features of work which are distinctive to this artist. Teaching is similar to this. Each teacher follows basic principles, and yet the work of each is different and significant. Pupils will receive something unusual from each teacher. There is need for much imagination in the field of art. A painting is an artist's impression of some event or situation. This impression is clear to him before he puts it on canvas. Without imagination there would be only landscapes, portraits, and still life in the art galleries. Imagination has caused the artists of the world to put into tangible expression their feelings and emotions.

The teacher must have imagination also. He must see more in the classroom on Sunday than he actually sees with his physical eyes. He needs to see housewives, teachers, missionaries, lawyers, doctors, preachers, deacons, farmers, and leaders in other professions. If he does not see young people as the future leaders of his community, he lacks this qualification for effective teaching.

At best, there is enough discouragement almost any Sunday to cause a teacher to consider resigning his class. But the use of imagination will cause him to see greater possibilities in his material and craftsmanship.

2. *The Expression of Friendship*

When teaching is thought of as the expression of friendship, the teacher is not primarily concerned with storing away factual information to pass on to the pupil at the proper time. He is more concerned in being a friend and participating in a fellowship of learning. Information is basic to learning, but the "deep-freeze" idea of storing it up emphasizes possessing knowledge more than using it. Instead of making preparation just to pass on information, the teacher prepares so that he may share his knowledge and experience with the pupils as they need it and ask for it. He thinks in terms of how he may create a desire for new information and experience when his pupils do not seem to realize their needs.

The teacher will encourage the class members to share their knowledge and experience with him. This is one of the ways the teacher learns. Young people have much to share. They are happy in sharing it and they learn thereby.

To the young person, a real teacher is not a "know-it-all." He is impressed with the teacher's superior knowledge of the subject, but he prefers to think of his teacher as a true friend, ready to join at any time in a quest for truth. This willingness to learn on the part of the teacher will prove a great asset in getting others to learn.

The teacher must be more mature and should have more knowledge and experience than those who are taught. Yet one of his main tasks is to reduce this difference in knowledge and experience between himself and his pupils even while he, himself, continues to grow in wisdom and maturity. Teaching would cease if this difference was canceled completely. This is one of the major reasons for continuous work by the teacher. One of the greatest gifts a person has to offer is that of his own friendship. This is more necessary and vital than material gifts. Someone has said there are three types of teachers: the forgiven, the forgotten, and the remembered. The ones who are remembered are the ones who take a personal interest in their pupils.

Friendship which develops in the experience of learning is the basis of friendship for life. Next to family ties, there are no greater ties than those formed in the classroom. A Chinese student in expressing this friendship for his teacher, quoted this Chinese proverb, "Once my teacher, always my father."

Since the teacher has Christ as his Friend in this fellowship of learning, it will be easy for the members to become friends of Christ also.

3. *Helping Another to Learn*

It is not enough for the teacher to study and learn for himself. This is only a part of the teaching process. Much of his study should be directed toward how to put his pupils to work at the same learning activities which engage his attention.

Some teachers admit they do not understand the true nature of teaching when they make such a statement as, "My pupils won't study, so I am having to try to put as much into the lesson period as possible." Pupils will never learn if the teacher attempts to learn for them. Imagine a high-school or college teacher assuming such an attitude!

Members may not be interested in Bible study, but they are interested in something. The teacher must discover what those interests are and use them to awaken an interest in Bible study and Christian living. Teaching is setting the stage for learning and planning so that learning situations will arise. If pupils do not see the values of the activities and experiences suggested by the teacher, they will not be attracted to participate in them.

Discovering how to unlock and open the closed doors of the young person's inner life is one of the most stimulating and exciting experiences in the world. It is in this situation that teaching becomes such a thrilling experience. A pupil who will not attend the class regularly, nor study, nor take any interest in the work of the class will prove to be a challenging subject to the genuine teacher. It is the teacher who misunderstands the true meaning of teaching who will desire to drop his name from the roll.

4. *Securing Participation*

It is important for young people in the Sunday school to secure Bible knowledge. But the principal reason for teaching Bible truth is not to have the pupils repeat it to the teacher. The purpose is for them to appropriate this truth and make it a part of life and conduct. They need to understand the ideals of the Christian faith so that they may keep them clearly in view as guides to right living. They also need to share in activities and experiences in which they may actually apply these ideals to concrete life experiences.

It is generally understood that one learns more when he participates in the activities of his class. The lesson is not the Bible passage or printed lesson helps alone. The lesson is these plus the activities and experiences of pupils upon which the Bible truth has a bearing.

The teacher then must arrange for his pupils to have the kind of experiences which will help them understand how to live as Christians and cause them to desire to live in this way. If experiences take place for which the teacher has not planned, he strives to use them in such a way as to insure that the pupils will learn something worth while from them.

Activity does not apply simply to the physical. Some teachers seem to feel that learning activity means mainly motor activity, so they plan as many things as possible to keep pupils busy with their hands and feet. Obviously physical activity is more desirable in teaching children than in teaching young people.

Participation, as set forth in this discussion, refers mainly to mental and emotional responses. Young people have the capacity for critical thinking. The teacher should strive to make every session of the class thought-provoking. He need not attempt anything startling or sensational in order to get his members to think. Sensationalism is not necessary, for nothing is more powerful than an idea. Learning takes place when pupils engage in considering, discussing, analyzing, and understanding ideas to meet a felt need.

It has been estimated that at best a person uses only about 10 per cent of his brain cells. Teaching is putting more and more of these unemployed cells to work.

Participation also calls for emotional responses. During a lesson period many emotional reactions occur. Some of these reactions may be fear, distrust, resentment, love, joy, or sympathy. There is a strong relationship between religion and the emotions. To arouse them and channel their expression properly is a legitimate objective for every teacher. Securing an emotional response should never be attempted as an end in itself but as a means of motivating learning and right conduct.

The Bible deals realistically with life situations. The experiences of men and women in the Bible call forth reactions from the members of the class. In studying the life of Simon Peter the members will find themselves condemning him for his actions in one experience, sympathizing with him in another, and admiring him in yet another. As they do this, they are doing more than learning the factual information regarding his life. They are building up emotional attitudes which will help them in making right choices later.

A teacher, then, helps pupils do things themselves. He arranges for them to participate in activities which may lead them to change and grow. He will put them to work, keep them at work, and work with them. He will lose them if they are not used.

III. Teaching Not Confined to the Classroom

In the preceding chapter the influence of the teacher's character, conduct, and conversation was pointed out. By his contacts with his members and his manner of life during the week he will exert a greater influence than he will on Sunday. If he lives at his best during the week, what he teaches on Sunday will possess greater influence.

1. *The General Life of the Church*

But the general life of the Sunday school and the church itself provides many learning opportunities. Often a church business meeting offers positive opportunity to practice "love thy neighbour as thyself." Such a meeting is a more powerful teaching instrument than memorizing the commandment.

A church may have the name "missionary" over its door, but if a small fraction of the church's funds has been contributed to missions, this expresses more profoundly than words what the church is really teaching about missions. There is real teaching when a Sunday school becomes the place where Christianity is demonstrated, rather than the place where teachers simply talk about it.

2. *Experiences in Home and Community*

Experiences which young people have in their homes, in their immediate communities, in school, and at work all form a part of the classroom of life. They learn from all these experiences, and what they learn is both good and bad for them. The more a teacher succeeds in getting young people to carry the teachings of Christ into all the areas of their lives, the more he will help them in learning to live the Christian life.

IV. THE SIGNIFICANCE OF CHRISTIAN TEACHING

Christian teaching is significant because it deals with life. Christian growth begins with conversion experience.

1. *Born to Grow*

Man is separated from God by sin. His supreme need is salvation. Man cannot save himself. Salvation which must come from another source has been provided in the person of Christ, our Saviour.

The principal objective of every teacher is to lead each unsaved pupil into a personal acceptance of faith in Christ.

Christ said to Nicodemus, "Ye must be born again" (John 3:7). This statement in itself implies growth. The birth of a child means a period of dependence upon his parents for love, care, and security until such time as he is mature enough to make decisions for himself.

In the spiritual realm this is no less true. These "new-born babes" must have "the sincere milk of the word" that they "may grow thereby" (1 Peter 2:2). Every new Christian, no matter what his age, needs instruction and guidance in the Christian life. Christ thought so because he gave much of his time to teaching new converts.

2. *Attaining Spiritual Maturity*

Christians will grow if they are expected to grow and are encouraged to do so. Teaching benefits everyone, but especially the immature Christian. In fact, it is the means of inducing growth. This growth is accelerated if the Christian becomes interested and puts forth effort for himself.

It is not only important for the new Christian to have the proper start in his Christian development, but this growth should continue to full maturity. Arrested development is one of the problems of most church members. There are too many grown babies in the church's membership. Paul wrote, "When I was a child, I spake as a child, I understood as a child, I thought as a child: but when I became a man, I put away childish things" (I Cor. 13:11). Too few Christians can say this.

Sometime ago, in an Adult union, a man arose and with an air of extreme nervousness made his way to the front of the room. He was a large man standing over six feet in height and weighing over two hundred pounds. When he reached the speaker's stand, he nearly collapsed on it; fortunately it was strong enough to support his weight. He braced himself and pushed his body up to its full height. As he trembled from head to foot, he began to speak. In substance he said: "I have been a Christian for eighteen years and have never prayed or spoken in public during this time. I have been afraid to do it. But I felt if I ever intended to do it, I should get started. So, when I was asked to be on the program, I made up my mind I was going to do it if it killed me." For a few moments it seemed as if it might. But he recovered from his fright and went on to complete his assignment very acceptably.

The response to this demonstration was immediate and unanimous. Before he sat down, all the members had expressed their encouragement and pleasure.

Later this man became a Sunday school teacher and deacon in his church. This eighteen-year-old baby took his first step and, after doing so, not only started walking but now is almost running in his Christian development. This is another testimony to the importance of educating and training converts so that they may grow in grace and leadership ability.

As a person's knowledge, ideals, and concepts are enlarged, he has every reason to desire to grow. There can be little growth apart from these new horizons. Regular study of the Bible provides the spiritual food for attaining maturity.

3. *The Promise of Christ's Presence*

Not only did Christ teach, but he promised he would be with those who taught in obedience to his command. Much of the emphasis of the Great Commission is upon teaching: "teach all nations, baptizing them" [the dramatic method of teaching], and "teaching them to observe all things whatsoever I have commanded you" (Matt. 28:19–20). To the one who obeys these commands Christ promised, "Lo, I am with you alway."

Christ knew that teaching was necessary to the success of the gospel enterprise and has promised to bless those who do it.

Each rising generation must be won and taught. The Christian message of faith and hope could be lost in any generation which went untaught. This means that every church, in order to be faithful to Christ's command, must support an adequate program of teaching. It means also, that the church which does will have the power and presence of Christ in accomplishing its task.

V. WHEN HAS A TEACHER TAUGHT?

Every teacher would like to know when he has really taught. Certainly a teacher has not taught every time he thinks he has.

1. *Difficult to Determine*

A teacher may complete a lesson period as he has planned. The pupils listened well, there was no disturbance. He was not interrupted by anyone entering the room after he began. He closed his lesson on time, using the illustration as he had planned. Then several members stopped as they left the classroom to say, "I enjoyed your lesson today." But has the teacher taught? Perhaps so and perhaps not. One cannot tell simply by how he feels about it nor by what the pupils say. It is often true that a teacher has done his best teaching when he feels most discouraged over his efforts.

2. *The Best Evidence*

The best indication of the teacher having taught is found in the evidences of changes in the lives of his pupils.

If a learner understands, he has been taught. If he sees the significance of new truth, not only in a general way, but in the way it applies to him; if he sets up ideals of conduct and behavior in terms of Bible standards and determines to live by them, the teacher has taught.

If these commitments last not for a few days or weeks but for years, the teaching of the teacher is effective. He has taught.

A salesman has not sold something until a customer has bought it. Neither has a teacher taught until a pupil appropriates the truth for himself.

FOR FURTHER STUDY

1. Evaluate the statement, "Put them to work, keep them at work, work with them."
2. Think of the new Christians in your class. Are they developing spiritually? What can you do to influence them to grow.
3. Have you claimed the promise of Christ's presence with you as you teach? What may the teacher do to experience more of the presence of Christ?

CHAPTER 3

I. YOUNG PEOPLE DIFFER

    1. Heredity
    2. Environment
    3. Age and Maturity

II. YOUTH, THE PEAK OF DEVELOPMENT

    1. Abundant Physical Energy
    2. Pronounced Intellectual Ability

III. YOUTH, A TIME OF CRITICAL ADJUSTMENTS

    1. Becoming Free from Home Restraints
    2. Completing Formal Training
    3. Entering upon a Vocation
    4. Attaining Economic Independence
    5. Achieving Citizenship Status
    6. Serving in the Armed Forces
    7. Dating and Courting
    8. Establishing Their Own Homes
    9. Formulating a Religious Faith and Life Philosophy

IV. YOUNG PEOPLE MUST BE UNDERSTOOD

    1. The Teacher Taking the Initiative
    2. The Teacher Remaining Objective in His Evaluation

V. YOUTH, A CHALLENGE TO ITS LEADERSHIP

3

Those We Would Teach

Then Jesus beholding him loved him
(Mark 10:21)

WHEN ONE BECOMES the teacher of a Young People's class, he accepts the responsibility of guiding the growth of a group of differing personalities. Although they are in the same "class," the teacher will soon discover they are not alike.

I. YOUNG PEOPLE DIFFER

Young people differ in general appearance, height, weight, color of hair and eyes, physical energy and strength, intelligence, social attitudes, and religious interest. If a teacher should decide to classify the members of his class in these different ways, he would find varying degrees of difference in each classification. These differences may be traced to several influences.

1. *Heredity*

The parents and grandparents of these young people contribute most to these differences. Some families show tendencies to height, while others have the opposite tendencies. Some have high intelligence, while others have average or below average intelligence. Some are well-balanced and controlled, while others are emotionally unstable and excitable.

Capacities for achievement in certain areas are inherited. Thus abilities in the fields of art, literature, mu-

31

sic, and leadership differ with individuals. The teacher should recognize these talents and seek to utilize them.

2. *Environment*

The conditions in the home and neighborhood make their influence felt upon young people. If a young person has been shielded and protected as a child, most likely he will be dependent upon his parents and friends as a young person. If he has been the center of attention, has had everything he has wanted, and has never known hardship, he may be self-centered and overbearing.

Friends are most influential at this age. If a young person associates with those who indulge in questionable amusements, and has not developed self-control, he will need a strong emphasis on Christian living.

On the other hand, if he has had opportunities for the expression of his own personality in the right environment, with only the amount of parental direction necessary, he will be the type of personality who may be relied upon for leadership in the class.

3. *Age and Maturity*

There are marked differences in the seventeen-year-old and the nineteen-year-old, and in the nineteen-year-old and the twenty-one-year-old. In fact, each year brings its own differences. In the Sunday schools where there is only one class for all young men, and one class for all young women, 17–24, the teacher has an even greater problem of meeting individual needs than the teacher who has a class of members of one age.

Age and maturity are not synonymous. Often a young person of seventeen is more mature than a young person of twenty-four. Much depends upon the experiences he has had and his reactions to them. If he has had responsibility, has had to make choices and decisions, and has learned to think for himself, he will have matured beyond those of his own age. Married young people with the new responsibilities of homemaking mature more rapidly as a group than young people who are single. Their differences in maturity and interests make it important to have separate classes and departments for them where there are sufficient possibilities.

Serving in the armed forces also accelerates maturity. Facing temptations and dangers, and making decisions without benefit of parental counsel, make it necessary for one to assume responsibility for his own actions. When young men and women are in combat or under any conditions where living becomes hazardous, their need for maturity is intensified. When they return to their churches, they often feel out of place with their associates. It is vital that they be understood and dealt with individually.

Thus a Young People's class is composed of individuals who must be understood in the light of their parents, their homes, their ages, and their experiences.

II. Youth, the Peak of Development

Although full maturity will come in adulthood, young people experience their prime in physical energy and intellectual vigor. Those who teach young people realize at once the abundant resources with which they work. Young people have no limits to enthusiasm and energy once they are challenged. If they enjoy their activities, they will invest time and effort in making them succeed.

If they are encouraged to be creative and original in their thinking, they will respond with genuine interest, putting their best thought into their work.

These things are possible because of the physical en-

ergy and intellectual powers of young people. Every
teacher should know these characteristics so that he may
utilize them in his work with this age group.

1. *Abundant Physical Energy*

It is in this age range that physical energy reaches its
peak. By the age of eighteen the skeletal growth is complete, although some growth continues in the bones
and teeth until the age of twenty-five.

Thus physical energy which was needed for growth is
now released for activity. Athletes are at their best in
their early twenties. This is the reason the armed forces
are anxious to have young people of these ages. They not
only spend enormous amounts of energy, but they have
great recuperative powers. Unless this energy can be cap-
tured for the work of the class, it will find some expression which will defeat the teacher.

2. *Pronounced Intellectual Ability*

Some believe a person achieves his intellectual majority at sixteen or seventeen, although he is at his best as a
student between the years of twenty and twenty-four.

During these years one's mind is as restless as one's
body. Because of increased ability to deal with ideas and
the discovery of new knowledge, the young person is
evaluating previous knowledge and experience. What he
accepted as a child through confidence in parents and
teachers, he is now seeking to make his own through
reason and analysis.

He is quick to apprehend, his mind is a question mark,
and he enjoys exploring for new truth. But in the earlier
years of this age group, one's judgment is not reliable and
he tires of thorough investigations.

There is a questioning of authority and a demand for

convincing evidence. The young person is interested in the explanation of things and is especially demanding of evidence.

Pupils vary in intellectual ability. Those who give evidence of greater ability should be given opportunities for extra work. Those who are below average should have assignments in keeping with their abilities.

III. YOUTH, A TIME OF CRITICAL ADJUSTMENTS

During the ages of 17 to 24 some of the most critical of all life adjustments are being made.

1. *Becoming Free from Home Restraints*

In modern life many young people have known little if any parental direction. Large numbers of them have had to shift for themselves during childhood, and many have been pushed out upon society in early adolescence.

But where young people lead a normal life, they inevitably reach the time when they must go out from the parental roof. This time comes for many when they go away to a college or university. In doing so, a young person trades the customary quietude of his own home for the noise, excitement, and rather artificial life of a college dormitory.

For others, the breaking of old ties comes as they leave their home communities to enter the armed forces or seek work elsewhere.

Whenever it occurs, it is an experience which has a marked effect upon the young person. If he has been trained properly and is self-disciplined, there are few problems. If he is not prepared for experiences which follow, he may make choices which shall mean a wasted life. Teachers alert to these difficulties can offer invaluable guidance at this time.

2. Completing Formal Training

One's learning should continue throughout life, but experiences in the classroom are terminated for most young people by the age of twenty-four. Some withdraw from high school before completing their course of study. A larger number graduate from high school. A small percentage continue on to a college or university. A very limited number take work leading to advanced degrees.

Some who dropped out of school earlier realize the need of additional training and re-enter, thus completing their formal training.

Due to financial reasons some may delay their studies until they earn enough money to finance their college or university training.

Some whose classroom activities were interrupted by military duty complete their education after they are discharged from the service.

Thus in the same Young People's class one may have members representing various phases of educational preparation.

3. Entering upon a Vocation

This is the time when young people begin their life-work. To many it is not a vocation ("calling"). It is only a means of earning a living. In seeking a job one often enters into a work for life.

It is much better if a young person is qualified, trained, and able to choose a vocation where he may express his real abilities and talents.

Whatever his work may be, he should see in it the opportunities for making his contribution to his fellow man.

He needs a Christian interpretation of work and an understanding of its importance to him as well as to others. Even though he works with a machine in what may be a meaningless operation, he needs to see something significant in such a task.

He should be guided, before reaching the time of employment, in understanding the many vocations which are open to young people. He should know something of the demand for workers in these fields. In certain groups of young people there is a tendency to choose from a limited number of vocations which may be overcrowded. A young person should be led to see his own strength and weakness, his aptitudes for certain vocations, and his negative qualities for others.

This does not mean he would enter only those vocations for which he has positive talents and abilities. But he should enter his vocation with definite knowledge as to the price he must pay and the handicaps he must overcome. As far as it is humanly possible, he should be guided into a vocation where a fair amount of success is possible. Many who have achieved the greatest success have had to overcome great handicaps in themselves and their environment to do so. Young people need to know that with God's help it is possible to do this.

Each young person should be led to see that any vocation needs a trained worker. Helping young people to desire and accomplish the proper training is the privilege of every young people's teacher.

4. *Attaining Economic Independence*

The normal young person desires to have money of his own so he can be independent in its use. In fact, it is in the economic area that the feeling of adolescent independence is so pronounced. As a rule, this independence begins with part-time work, which is more easily secured by young men than by young women. From such a beginning there is gradual progression toward full-time employment and complete independence.

If he earns his own money, there is the logical feeling that he is free to spend it as he desires. This may lead to a greater sense of independence and freedom. It may also lead to conflicts with parents if the young person is still living at home.

Often, a young person must secure work in order to help support his family. This means giving up plans for his own education, marriage, and the vocation he desires to enter. In this sense he is not economically free. It will be necessary for him to adjust to these conditions and postpone his plans. A teacher of such a young person should do everything possible to encourage him and assist him in realizing his goals.

Earlier teaching regarding the stewardship of life and money will have its influence at this time. Stewardship should be taught at this age, but if it is based upon previous teaching, it will prove more effective.

In this area as in all other areas of adolescent growth, the parents and teachers must prove themselves to be friends rather than dictators.

5. *Achieving Citizenship Status*

At some time during the years from 18 to 21, young people in the various states are given the right to vote. This means, according to law, that these young people have reached a point in maturity where they have a right to help choose those who make the laws and otherwise lead in the affairs of state. Such recognition adds to their feeling of independence and self-sufficiency.

Youth should be taught the importance of the ballot in a democracy and encouraged to exercise the privilege of voting. They should be led to vote intelligently.

6. *Serving in the Armed Forces*

Military service is an experience common to many young men. To a less degree it is experienced by young women. The need for young people in the armed forces varies with the international situation. In times of war all young men are subject to the draft, and only those with reasons which are permissible are exempt. Young women, while not drafted, are recruited in large numbers.

In times of peace only such numbers are sought as are needed to guarantee the nation's safety. But for a long while to come, the demand will continue and large numbers of young people will be needed. Some will serve only for the time required, while others will make a career of military service.

Young people need preparation for facing the temptations which life in the armed forces carries with it. More and more the churches are learning the value of giving this preparation and of using the Young People Away department to keep in contact with young people when they enter upon military duty.

7. *Dating and Courting*

At the beginning of adolescence, interest in the opposite sex is very strong. Girls are interested in boys because they are boys, and boys are interested in girls because they are girls. One definition of adolescence is: "When a Boy Scout becomes a girl scout." Soon this general interest gives way to interest in a few, and finally only one. The book with names, addresses, and telephone numbers is gradually revised until it contains only the choice few or one.

Throughout adolescence the group spirit is very strong. School spirit, the teen-age "gangs" of the cities, fraternities and sororities of high schools and colleges, and many other factors attest this fact.

Since young people choose their dates from their circle of acquaintances and friends, forming right friendships during this period is extremely important.

For the first few years, there is interest in dating different ones before "going steady." There is an advantage in this since it gives young people contacts with different types of personalities. Understanding these differences enables them to be better prepared for the selection of a life companion.

It is important for young people to know that the kind of persons they are will determine the kind of friends and companions they have. Therefore, if one wants to marry a person who is stable, well-balanced, industrious, thrifty, and religious, he should attempt to be that kind of person himself.

Someone has advised those who believe in love at first sight to take a second look. It is not enough to look at the person only. The second look should consider other members of the family also. In a real sense, one not only marries a person, he marries a family as well. "Whether we like it or not, we marry our relatives. The unsuspecting bride and groom may soon find out that the question of an antiknock in their automobile motor is not half as much a problem as an aunty knocking at the door." [1]

The teacher can render a genuine service in helping young people to know the real meaning of love and romance. The concept given by popular songs and the movies is inaccurate. One does not "fall in love" but achieves love by giving oneself without reservation to the person of his choice. The chief tests of love are absence, time, and companionship.

---

[1] From *Youth and the Homes of Tomorrow* by Edwin T. Dahlberg, copyright 1934 by the Judson Press. Used by permission.

8. *Establishing Their Own Homes*

A larger proportion of young people today are married than ever before. Many of them are living in apartments or houses apart from their own immediate families. But there are large numbers of them who must, of necessity, live with their parents or other relatives.

In addition to the adjustments which the two must make with each other, there are often the additional and sometimes difficult adjustments to make with other members of the family. These and other difficulties frequently place a heavy strain upon domestic relationships. Added to this is the lack of knowledge and preparation which so often characterizes marriage.

Churches are beginning to sense the importance of preparation for marriage and are offering greater guidance in this area to their young people. Conferences are conducted for young people who are contemplating marriage and for those who are married. Pastors are preaching special messages to prepare young people for this relationship. They are counseling those who are to be married as they confer regarding their plans for marriage.

A book especially written for young people is *Tomorrow You Marry* by Joe W. Burton. It sets forth a Christian approach to courtship and marriage. This book is in category 3 of the Church Study Course. It should be taught periodically to all young people of the church.

After marriage, much help may be given to young people through planning activities to meet their special needs. If classes and departments are provided for married young people, the teachers can make special provision for teaching and for the social life of the classes.

When a child is born, the teacher should secure the

co-operation of the pastor and the Cradle Roll superintendent in ministering to the family. If the child is brought to Sunday school, immediately the Nursery department will accept this ministry. Such contacts will prove helpful in undergirding home life and in meeting the needs of young parents. Every home should receive a copy of *Home Life* each month.

9. *Formulating a Religious Faith and Life Philosophy*

With increased intellectual powers, wider social contacts, and greater experience, young people are making religious faith a personal thing. Seeing the inequalities and injustices in life calls for a re-evaluation of such great themes as the nature of man, sin, salvation, a Christian social order, and the ultimate purposes of living.

It is not unnatural for young people to have religious doubts during this time. This is especially true if they are in contact with those who ridicule their Christian beliefs. Each one is inclined to feel his experience of doubting is an unusual one. It helps him to know that this experience of questioning is somewhat general among young people. If doubt is harbored, it may lead to feelings of guilt and remorse. It may even alienate him from the church. The teacher must do what he can to settle such questions.

Young people should be led to feel perfect freedom in discussing problems of doubt privately or in the class. It is in this area that Sunday school teachers may make one of their greatest contributions.

Many young people have developed in such a way that they do not experience the questionings which appear in the minds of others. These may be used in class discussions for testimonies and information which will be of value to those who are still searching for truth.

IV. Young People Must be Understood

The previous discussion has been brief but as comprehensive as space would permit. Many books have been written on the psychology of adolescence, so there is much information available for those who work with young people. This discussion and the wealth of literature on the subject emphasize the need for understanding the ones we teach. If the teacher ever gets beyond generalities in his teaching, he must know the characteristics, experiences, interests, problems, and needs of his class members.

1. *The Teacher Taking the Initiative*

It is difficult for Sunday school teachers to accept responsibility for enlisting members. Some have said, "It seems the height of egotism to invite pupils to hear me teach." This is not a valid objection. The teacher is not primarily inviting the pupil to hear him. He is inviting him to join in regular Bible study in which the teacher as well as the member shall be learning.

In the Sunday school it is axiomatic that a teacher must not only make preparation for teaching, but also must enlist a class for Bible study. In this endeavor he is aided by the officers of the class.

Enlistment through personal invitation is the best means the teacher has for knowing his pupils. On Sunday in the class one may gain only partial information regarding the aims, ideals, and ambitions of each pupil. But in their homes or wherever they are visited, what they are thinking, feeling, and desiring comes to the surface. Thus visitation is really preparation for teaching. When the teacher is visiting, he is getting ready to teach.

The teacher is following Bible commands when he goes

out to enlist new members and learn more about the
needs of members already enrolled. In the Old Testament is the command, "Gather the people together, . . .
that they may learn" (Deut. 31:12). In the New Testament, Christ commissioned his followers to "go . . . and
teach" (Matt. 28:19).

This is the method Christ used and left for his disciples
to follow. If the teacher says, "They know where the
church is, why should I go to visit them?" he should reread these two Bible passages until he is assured of God's
plan.

2. *The Teacher Remaining Objective in His Evaluation*

The teacher must not permit his love or sympathetic
understanding to keep him from forming a correct esti-
mate of the weaknesses and difficulties of his members.

If one truly loves young people, he will not be blind
to their defects. He must accept them as they are, knowing that in the companionship of Bible study, prayer, and
Christian service are the greatest opportunities for
growth and maturity.

V. YOUTH, A CHALLENGE TO ITS LEADERSHIP

Those who are led to work with young people are
fortunate. Where may one find the opportunities and
challenge so great?

This is a period of life in which some of the greatest
decisions are made. Young people are deciding for or
against education. They are seeking to find their places
in the work and service of the world. They are selecting
their life companions and establishing their homes. They
are deciding for or against Christ. They are either on
the road to maturity, happiness, and success or the road
to delinquency, crime, and defeat.

Since it is from this age group that such a large percentage of criminals comes, the teacher becomes one of the most significant persons in American life. Young people have the physical energy, intellectual ability, courage, and daring to be either spiritual leaders or criminals.

Young people's teachers have the answer to youth's need in the gospel of Jesus Christ. They are the bearers of the "good news" at a time when youth is eager for a challenge. It is possible that they are the only exponents of genuine love which many young people know. Sunday school teachers may be the only ones who show a sincere interest and desire to help the young person realize his cherished ambitions in life. To be able to assist some young person to reach his maximum stature as a Christian should provide enough motivation to keep any teacher working consistently at his task.

FOR FURTHER STUDY

1. Write down the names of the two members of your class who are most unlike. Indicate in brief lists the physical, mental, social, and spiritual differences of these two members.
2. Select at random two members of your class. Think seriously of the critical adjustments each is making to life situations.
3. Look at the list of "critical adjustments" discussed in the chapter. Which three in the list seem to predominate among the members of your class?
4. Do you know the members of your class well enough to evaluate the needs of each one objectively? If not, what can you do to secure the information you need?
5. Are you challenged by the young people in your class? What challenges you the most?

CHAPTER 4

4

Aims in Teaching Young People

That the man of God may be perfect, throughly furnished unto all good works (2 Tim. 3:17)

RECENTLY, the writer was a guest for dinner in the home of an Intermediate department superintendent, who is an expert marksman. He has many guns equipped with telescopic sights. In the basement of his home he has a rifle range and loads his own shells as a hobby.

During the dinner he informed me that a class of boys in his department was coming over for target practice that night. After dinner we went downstairs, where he set up a target and fired several practice shots to make sure the gun sight was properly adjusted. He then set up as a target a card with its edge toward him. Taking careful aim, he promptly clipped it in half with a bullet from the gun.

Since the class of boys had not come, he asked me whether I would like to try my skill with the gun. He gave me a few preliminary instructions, and then I found myself looking through the telescopic sight, trying to find the thin edge of another card he had set up. When it was located, it seemed near enough to touch. When it was centered in the gun sight, I fired. You guessed it—I missed! Even with the most scientific equipment, clear instructions, and aiming directly at the target, I missed!

To make it worse, when the class and its teacher arrived later, several of the Intermediate boys clipped the cards with their first shots.

Everyone knows that aiming a gun is necessary. But

not everyone knows that having an aim for teaching is just as important.

A person's purpose, or goal, indicates what he expects to do about a given thing. In the Sunday school, teaching aims indicate what one desires the outcomes of his work to be. When a teacher sets up a goal for his teaching, he seeks to determine in advance what his teaching is to accomplish.

If one misses a target when aiming directly at it, how much farther will he miss if he fails to aim at all! A teacher "just teaching" will accomplish something because the Word of God has tremendous power in and of itself (Heb. 4:12). But teaching will accomplish much more if it is done by a skilled workman who knows what he is attempting to do.

I. JESUS' AIMS FOR TEACHING

The "Lesson" on the Mount, Matthew 5–7, indicates the great objectives of the master Teacher. He was aiming at regenerated lives and growth in Christlikeness. There is no statement anywhere which so clearly presents what Christ came to accomplish through his earthly ministry. If a teacher reads these chapters with this in mind, he will have a clear idea of what he is to be, and what he is to lead his members to become.

Christ stated his principal aim in this manner, "I am come that they might have life, and that they might have it more abundantly" (John 10:10). His main purpose was to live life above the purely physical plane and introduce man to the greater spiritual values.

He taught Nicodemus how this new life was to begin, "Marvel not that I said unto thee, Ye must be born again" (John 3:7).

He accepted Simon Peter as he was but challenged him

to become great, "Thou art Simon the son of Jona: thou shalt be called Cephas, which is by interpretation, A stone" (John 1:42).

II. THE VALUES OF AIMS

Having aims for teaching is valuable in many ways. Some of the most important values are presented to encourage the selection and use of teaching aims.

1. *Aims Give Direction*

It is important to have a sense of direction in learning. A man driving down a highway at seventy miles an hour may be going in the wrong direction. He needs a map which will indicate his destination and how to reach it.

The late G. S. Hopkins, former Sunday school secretary of Texas, used to tell of traveling for a hundred miles before he discovered that he did not have his engagement book and did not know where he was going. Entering a filling station for the purpose of calling his office, he discovered that the attendant was a Baptist who had heard announcements of Dr. Hopkins' coming and could direct him to the proper place for the meeting.

If a teacher knows what he is seeking to accomplish, he knows how to plan to reach his goal.

2. *Aims Give Confidence to the Teacher and Members*

Having an aim creates a feeling of confidence. Teaching and learning become significant, for there is something to be accomplished. There is far more involved in teaching next Sunday's lesson than the fact that it is the one for next Sunday.

A teacher stepped from his classroom one Sunday morning muttering: "I've done it! I've done it!"

The general superintendent, standing near by, heard him and asked, "What have you done?"

The teacher said: "I've taught next Sunday's lesson to-day! All my life I have been afraid I would do it, and now I've done it! I've done it!"

The superintendent then asked, "What did the class think of it?"

"Oh," the teacher replied, "they haven't found it out yet!"

Certainly any group engaged in the process of learning should have a better sense of direction than this.

3. Aims Prevent Wasted Effort

Having definite aims will guide in concentrating upon the main task at hand. There are certain things which are more important for a class to learn than others. The effective teacher must be selective and make every moment count toward the important materials, activities, and experiences. Much time is lost in trying to teach persons what they already know. One does not teach another what he already knows. He teaches what is new to his class member. Aims which cause the teacher to get into new and challenging areas of thought will save his time and keep his pupils from being frustrated.

4. Aims Guide in Selecting Activities and Materials

When a teacher knows what he is trying to accomplish, he can choose intelligently the activities and materials to accomplish his purpose. He will plan to magnify and utilize certain portions of the printed lesson passage more than other portions. He will search for additional materials to supplement what is found in the lesson helps. He may turn to the hymnal, a picture, an incident from history, or some story from contemporary life for the additional material needed.

The type of procedure in the classroom may be selected more intelligently if there is purpose. The teacher may raise questions, have a discussion, lecture, or use the chalkboard as a means of accomplishing his purpose. Such a selection will be made intelligently if the teacher knows why the selection is being made.

5. *Aims Aid in Measuring the Results of Teaching*

When the teacher knows what he is trying to do, it is much simpler to determine whether or not he is doing it. By shooting at a target one may know whether he hits it or not.

If the purpose of a lesson is to lead each member of the class to become a tither, one may measure the immediate success of his lesson by the number of members who begin to tithe and continue to practice it.

The class may need much teaching on this subject. Several lessons over a period of many months may be necessary before much response is noted. If the first lesson elicits surprise, questions, or resentment, the teacher will be able to measure what that lesson accomplished and may proceed in his planning from that point. At any rate he will be able to evaluate each lesson from the standpoint of pupil interest and response.

III. Types of Aims

There are two principal types of aims: the ultimate and the immediate.

1. *The Ultimate*

By ultimate aims are meant the general statements of outcomes to be accomplished by religious teaching and training. Such aims cover the entire life span of each individual. Those who work with all age groups should have them in mind as they teach.

In one sense they are unattainable. As a pupil grows, the teacher must set new aims for teaching him. No teacher must permit a pupil to catch up with the goals he has set for him. This idea is involved in the statement "Hitch your wagon to a star." The star is so remote that one can never really hitch his wagon to it. But the fact that one sets a high aim aids him in achieving far more than if his aim were lower. The persons who have ceased to grow are those who have caught up with their ideals.

One can never be as Christlike, or know as much about the Bible, or be as considerate of his neighbor as he ought to be; but he should be kept working toward these objectives.

2. *The Immediate*

Immediate aims are the specific steps in the process of progressing toward the ultimate aims. It is important to have in mind the kind of adult one wants the young person to become. But the kind of young person he is now will determine the kind of adult he becomes.

An ultimate aim of the Sunday school teacher should be to lead his pupil to a thorough knowledge of the Bible. Immediate steps in the process may be to lead the pupil to purchase a Bible, study each lesson each week, bring his Bible to class with him, participate in the daily Bible readings of the Training Union, take part in Bible Study Week each January, and use his Bible in personal soul-winning. It is only in these and other ways the pupil will move toward a mastery of the content of the Bible.

Immediate aims are necessary, for they afford the best way of interpreting the ultimate aims to class members. The Chinese have a proverb, "The journey of a thousand miles begins with a single step." The teacher must have great objectives for his pupils, but he must begin with these pupils where they are and lead them step by step toward these goals.

IV. GUIDING FACTORS IN SELECTING AIMS

Several factors serve to guide the teacher in choosing aims for his pupils.

1. *Knowledge of the Characteristics of the Age Group*

Knowing young people as a group will prove helpful to the teacher. Certain physical, social, intellectual, and spiritual characteristics are observable to all who study this age group. These characteristics differ from those of children and adults. Thus young people must be guided differently. They will respond to teaching and leadership which is in keeping with their development.

The teacher using this information will plan aims which will cause the young people to feel they are being considered in the teacher's plans.

2. *Knowledge of Each Member*

It is important to know the characteristics of young people, but it is more important to know each young person who is a member of one's class. It is at this point that teaching becomes most helpful. The teacher has many sources of information concerning the members of his class.

(1) *The study of records.*—If the Sunday school has adequate records, it will provide each teacher with a class roll and information regarding the name, address, age, and spiritual condition of each member. With this in hand, each teacher may then study the Six Point Record System report of each member every week. This will give the teacher a great amount of usable information. The study of the pupil's record each week will guide the teacher in knowing what his teaching aims should be.

(2) *Personal visitation.*—The teacher, by making con-

tacts with the class members between Sundays, will discover much which will prove helpful in knowing what direction his teaching should take. In these contacts many of the member's problems emerge, and his interests and ambitions are made known. This will guide the teacher in determining both ultimate and immediate goals for his teaching.

This is one of the basic reasons why men should teach young men, and women should teach young women. It is through these informal weekday contacts that teachers receive information which may be directed toward the solution of personal problems and difficulties.

(3) *Class discussion.*—Expressions of members in class will indicate many needs to the teacher. In order to teach effectively, a teacher must know what his pupils are thinking, feeling, and desiring. If he will plan for class participation, he will soon know the areas of need represented in his class. This will guide him in determining the direction of his teaching.

(4) *Informal contacts outside the class.*—The teacher should study young people through contacts at parties, picnics, athletic events, or in any other way where an atmosphere of fellowship and freedom exists. In this atmosphere there will be many opportunities for the members to express themselves freely and frankly. When members are uninhibited, they express their true thoughts and feelings. During such contacts what a person is becomes more apparent.

The teacher will not attempt to pry into the secret compartments of any life at any time. Certainly he should not take advantage of his position and learn information about each person simply for the sake of knowing something no one else knows. He should never violate a member's confidence by divulging information of a personal nature to others. The teacher seeks to understand his members so that he may plan to meet their needs through a constructive approach to Bible Study.

3. *Knowledge of the Lesson Material*

The very nature of the Bible Material will have a bearing on the teacher's aim. He must select from it what he feels is most significant for his pupils to learn. He should have a general aim for the teaching of the lessons for the quarter, established in advance through his preview study. Usually, he will group the quarter's lessons into smaller units, and determine his aim for each of these sub-units or groups, as well as for each lesson.

V. Some Basic Aims for the Teacher

As guiding principles, the teacher should keep in mind the following statement of general or ultimate aims.[1] They are stated for young people, but the aims are co-extensive with life, since they are never fully achieved.

1. *Christian Conversion*

Our aim is to lead each unsaved young person to a genuine experience of the forgiving and saving grace of God through Jesus Christ. This means helping each one:

(1) to become aware of the nature and prevalence of sin and to recognize God's judgment upon it;

(2) to realize his own sin and his consequent need of the salvation which God has provided in Christ;

(3) to turn from sin and commit himself to Jesus Christ, the Son of God, who gives complete salvation to all who trust him;

(4) to gain, after conversion, a growing sense of assurance as to the reality of that experience and its implications in terms of the lordship of Jesus.

2. *Church Membership*

Our aim is to guide each Christian young person into intelligent, active, and devoted membership in a New Testament church. This means helping each one:

---

[1] These aims are from *The Curriculum Guide,* 1960, (Convention Press) and are subject to revision.

(1) to unite with a church by baptism upon a personal profession of faith in Christ (if he has not already done so) ;

(2) to grow in understanding and appreciation of the meaning, purpose, faith, and practices of his church;

(3) to grow in loyalty to his church and the world program of Christ;

(4) to participate wholeheartedly in Christian service in and through the channels of his church;

(5) to transfer his church membership promptly when he changes his place of residence.

3. *Christian Worship*

Our aim is to help each young person make Christian worship a vital and constant part of his expanding experience. This means helping each one:

(1) to develop a deepening understanding of the meaning and values of worship;

(2) to develop a growing appreciation of all the elements that make for meaningful worship, both private and corporate;

(3) to develop and maintain the practice of daily individual worship, including the devotional reading of the Bible, meditation, and prayer;

(4) to develop the habit of regular attendance upon the public services of his church and the ability to participate in them with understanding and appreciation;

(5) to encourage and to participate in experiences of family worship.

4. *Christian Knowledge and Conviction*

Our aim is to help each young person to grow toward mature Christian knowledge, understanding, and conviction. This means helping each one:

(1) With respect to the Bible—

    a. to recognize the Bible as a unique revelation from God and to accept its authority as supreme in matters of faith and conduct;

    b. to gain fuller understanding of the origins of the Bible, the history of its preservation, and the significance of the many translations and versions;

    c. to achieve an increasing knowledge of the content of the Bible and a growing understanding of the customs, geography, and history out of which the Bible came;

    d. to acquire a growing comprehension of how Bible truths apply to personal daily living, to family life, and to community and world problems;

    e. to commit choice passages to memory.

(2) With respect to the great realities of the Christian faith—

    a. to grow in understanding of the nature, attributes, and disposition of God;

    b. to grow in understanding of the nature of man, of sin and salvation, and of the varied elements of Christian experience;

c. to grow in understanding of the Christian concepts of personal righteousness and social responsibility;

d. to develop a growing conviction about the truth and finality of the Christian faith.

(3) With respect to the Christian movement—

a. to know something of the general outline of Christian history;

b. to learn some of the outstanding facts about other Christian groups and our common heritage with them;

c. to grow in understanding of present-day trends and issues in the Christian movement and to develop ability to evaluate their significance for his own life, his own church, and the cause of Christ throughout the world.

(4) With respect to his church and denomination—

a. to understand something of the history of Baptists;

b. to understand the distinctive features of Baptist doctrine and polity;

c. to grow in his understanding of the program, missionary outreach, problems, and needs of his church and denomination;

d. to develop worthy convictions about the doctrines and mission of Baptists and about his personal responsibility to his denomination.

5. *Christian Attitudes and Appreciations*

Our aim is to assist each young person in developing such Christian attitudes and appreciations that he will have a Christian approach to all of life. This means helping each one:

(1) Regarding God—

a. to reverence God, respect his commandments, and seek to know and do his will as the supreme good;

b. to love and trust the Heavenly Father, Jesus Christ as Lord and Saviour, and the Holy Spirit as ever-present counselor and source of power;

c. to develop a sense of gratitude to God for all his goodness.

(2) Regarding the meaning of existence—

a. to regard all existence as the expression of God's creative power, wisdom, and goodness;

b. to see himself in relation to all existence in such a way as to feel secure in the purpose and sovereignty of God;

c. to regard life as a trust from God to be used for his glory and the good of others;

d. to believe with confidence that the Bible and the Holy Spirit are his guides in making the best use of this life;

e. to believe that the main purposes of God for mankind are redemption and development in righteousness.

(3) Regarding self—

a. to realize that as a person created in the image of God, he is of infinite worth and has marvelous possibilities;

b. to realize that he stands in continuing need of forgiveness and strength from God;

c. to recognize that he possesses spiritual needs and capacities which only God can supply;

d. to acknowledge that his body is a divine trust to be cared for, to be protected from abuse, to be disciplined in habit, to be employed in honest labor, considerate service, and healthful recreation;

e. to dedicate all of his God-given abilities to the pursuit and achievement of worthy aims and to find the measure of their worthiness in the teachings of Jesus;

f. to have as his personal ideal the attainment of a mature, well-balanced Christian personality.

(4) Regarding others—

a. to cultivate an attitude of Christian love, the willingness to practice forgiveness, and the determination to apply Christian principles in all his relationships;

b. to accept responsibility for the influence of his life upon all people whom his life touches;

c. to develop wholesome attitudes toward other young people of the opposite sex;

d. to cultivate a sense of belonging to the human race as a whole;

e. to develop an attitude of Christian concern for the welfare of people of all cultures, social levels, and races;

f. to feel a concern for the salvation of all men everywhere and to accept the obligation to share the gospel and the blessings of the Christian faith;

g. to feel a responsibility to pass on to future generations the good in his social heritage enriched by his own contribution to it.

(5) Regarding the Bible and divine institutions—

a. to develop a growing love for the Bible and an appreciation of the relevance of Bible teaching to daily life;

b. to respect the divine nature and purpose of the church and to give it a place of sacred pre-eminence over all institutions of human origin;

c. to respect the ordinances of baptism and the Lord's Supper and to seek through the right observance of them to honor Christ;

d. to regard the Lord's Day as the Christian sabbath to be used to the honor of the risen Christ;

e. to accept the standards set by Christ and the New Testament for marriage and family life;

f. to respect the institution of civil government as being of divine appointment and accept the responsibilities of good citizenship.

(6) Regarding the present world—

a. to feel that the world as God made it is good and that all the resources of nature and the necessity to work are gifts of God designed for the enrichment of life;

b. to recognize that evil is a dominant force in the world order and that the Christian, while he must live in this world, is not to share its spirit nor indulge in its sins but is to resist evil and be a positive force for morality and justice;

    c. to develop a deepening consciousness of responsibility for the social order of which he is a part and to desire to make the best contribution he can to the improvement of social conditions and the creation of a more Christlike society.

6. *Christian Living*

Our aim is to guide each young person in developing habits and skills which promote spiritual growth and in applying Christian standards of conduct in every area of life. This means helping each one:

    (1) to live daily in vital fellowship with Jesus Christ, seeking always to bring the whole life under the direction of the Holy Spirit;

    (2) to engage regularly in serious Bible study and to use the Bible as a guide for life;

    (3) to understand the values of prayer and to practice prayer in daily experience;

    (4) to pattern all of his personal conduct in accordance with the teachings, spirit, and example of Jesus Christ;

    (5) to do all possible to make his home life Christian;

    (6) to refuse to enter into relations and participate in activities which compromise or violate New Testament principles;

    (7) to seek to apply Christian principles and standards of conduct to all social relationships.

7. *Christian Service*

Our aim is to lead each young person to make his maximum contribution to the cause of Christ. This means helping each one:

    (1) to seek and use opportunities to invest his talents and skills in Christian service;

    (2) to witness consistently to the truth and power of the Christian faith and to seek to win others to Jesus Christ;

    (3) to work faithfully for the building up of his church and to serve sacrificially in and through his church;

    (4) to give of his money, from worthy motives and according to biblical teaching, for the support of his church and its work;

    (5) to show compassion for persons in need and do deeds of helpfulness in his daily life;

    (6) to find God's will for his life, to prepare adequately for the vocation to which he is called, and to enter that vocation with a sense of dedication to Christian service;

    (7) to serve effectively as a member of a team and to serve without desire for self-glory;

    (8) to dedicate his total personality and resources to world missions as the means of carrying forward the redemptive undertaking of Jesus Christ;

(9) to join with others in co-operative action for the improvement of social conditions, the creation of a more Christian society, and the realization of God's purpose for mankind.

VI. FORMULATING THE AIM

Arriving at an aim for teaching is one of the most tedious and difficult steps in preparing to teach. Dr. John H. Jowett once indicated that the most difficult part of sermon preparation was to reduce to a sentence or two the purpose he desired to achieve through his sermon. This is true of teaching also. This explains why setting aims is so difficult for most teachers.

But the time spent in selecting an aim is one of the best investments a teacher makes. If this can be done prior to the weekly officers and teachers' meeting, all teachers may join in discussing the aims they have selected. Although all teachers study the same lesson material, the aim will differ with each class. However, the discussion of their aims will prove stimulating and helpful to each teacher. Following the meeting each teacher may restudy the statement of his aim and improve upon it.

It is only through constant practice that the teacher will become skilled in formulating aims for teaching. If the purpose is the acquisition of knowledge, he might state his aim in this manner, "To lead my pupils to understand (the truth of the lesson) so that they may be able to interpret it to others."

When the aim is to lift the ideals of class members, it might be stated in these words, "To lead each person to take the Christian ideals (advanced in next Sunday's study) and make them his guides in life decisions."

If the aim is to motivate conduct the teacher might formulate his aim as follows, "To lead each member to feel the importance of applying (the truth of the lesson) to the experiences of life."

VII. Evaluating Aims for Teaching

When aims are decided upon, they should be evaluated before they are accepted for use. Certain questions will help in this evaluation.

1. *Do the Aims Have Merit?*

Certainly the aims should be worthy. If the teacher and the class spend time in lesson preparation and discussion, the time invested should be directed toward the highest goals. The teacher should be sure he is dealing with the central truth of the lesson. He should be assured that in pursuing the aim he will arrive at something significant for his pupils.

2. *Can the Aims Be Attained?*

This question applies to the specific aims of the teacher. He should attempt something which he feels the members of the class may accomplish. Success will not be measured in terms of reaching fully each aim established. But the teacher must attempt what he and the class can do. If he is too ambitious and sets his aims too high, he will confuse and discourage his members.

3. *Are the Aims Related to Life Situations?*

The aims should be practical. They should offer help and direction for here and now. They should also offer solutions for life's problems in the future. Christ's teaching always dealt with life experiences. He used life situations for teaching and interpreted his teaching in terms of living.

4. *Do the Aims Have Spiritual Value?*

Aims should emphasize the highest spiritual values in lesson materials. The teacher should know the facts of

Bible history, geography, and customs, but he should not major upon these areas in Sunday school teaching. He should use his knowledge to help the pupils discover the spiritual significance of the Bible passage. The aim should plot a clear path to the doctrines of great spiritual importance, such as: sin, salvation, the virgin birth of Christ, the inspiration of the Scriptures, the right of each person to access to God, the privilege of church membership, the supreme worth of the human soul, and the need of the world for the gospel of Christ. The teacher's aim should be to lead pupils not only to grasp the meaning of such fundamental truths, but also to accept the implications for their personal lives. In every lesson there is some predominate spiritual theme. The teacher should never permit himself to become sidetracked by anything else.

FOR FURTHER STUDY

1. It would be an enriching experience to seek scriptural statements of teaching aims. List some areas which should be covered in aims, as has been done in the first column. After each, list one or more Scripture passages which state an aim in that area. Here is one such list, which you will wish to revise and expand:

Area	Scripture Passage
Concept of God	Matthew 22:37
Acceptance of Christ	John 14:6
Christlike Character	Matthew 5:48
Enlistment in Missions	Matthew 28:19
Church Loyalty	Acts 2:42
Christian Interpretation of Life	Colossians 1:17
Growth in Bible Knowledge	Luke 24:45
Good Family Adjustments	Exodus 20:12; Deuteronomy 6:4-9

2. Recently the Baptist Sunday School Board has formulated a statement of overarching objectives to guide its educational and editorial personnel. These basic statements underlie the objectives for young people discussed in this chapter. Consider the following condensed statement of the major objectives and discover how the specific aims for young people, as discussed on pages 55 to 60, relate to these over-all aims.

(1) To lead each person to a genuine experience of the forgiving and saving grace of God through Jesus Christ.

(2) To guide each person into intelligent, active, and devoted membership in a New Testament church.

(3) To help each person to make Christian worship a vital and constant part of his expanding experience.

(4) To help each person to know the Bible; the great realities of the Christian faith; the history and status of the Christian movement; and the history, distinctive beliefs, and practices of his own denomination; and to develop deep and abiding Christian convictions concerning all these matters.

(5) To assist each person in developing such Christian attitudes and appreciations in every area of experience that he will have a Christian approach to all of life.

(6) To guide each person in developing habits and in learning techniques which promote personal spiritual growth, and in accepting and applying Christian standards of personal and social conduct in every area of life.

(7) To guide each person to invest his talents and to develop skills in Christian service.[2]

3. Consider next Sunday's lesson. Formulate an aim for teaching it.

4. Evaluate this aim by using the suggested tests in the chapter. Should your aim be restated?

5. Suggest some values of frequent discussion of aims at the weekly officers and teachers' meeting.

---

[2] W. L. Howse, *The Church Staff and Its Work* (Nashville: Broadman Press, 1959), pp. 36-37.

CHAPTER 5

I. THE IMPORTANCE OF METHOD

II. FACTORS IN THE SELECTION OF METHOD

1. The Aim of the Teacher
2. The Nature of Lesson Materials
3. The General Environment of Teaching
4. The Previous Experience and Maturity of the Pupils
5. The Previous Experience and Skill of the Teacher

III. SOME METHODS OF TEACHING YOUNG PEOPLE

1. The Discussion Method
2. The Question and Answer or Recitation Method
3. The Lecture Method
4. The Story Method
5. The Combination Method

IV. VISUAL AIDS IN TEACHING

1. Values in Visual Aids
2. Principles in Using Visual Aids
3. Nonprojected Visual Aids
4. Projected Visual Aids

5

Methods of Teaching Young People

And he spake this parable unto them
(Luke 15:3)

JESUS was master Teacher in the use of method. Yet he did not use methods simply for the sake of using them. He used a method because no other way offered such an opportunity for accomplishing his purpose. He was never a slave to method but placed the need of his learners first.

Jesus often taught by informal conversation (John 3–4). One might note that in these experiences it was never beneath the dignity of Christ to teach one person. Some of the greatest recorded statements of Christ came in his conversations with only one individual.

Jesus told a story when it would help to make his meaning clear. The verse at the beginning of this chapter is taken from Luke 15. This chapter abounds in stories which are clear, dramatic, and moving. Each possesses tremendous teaching values.

Jesus lectured upon occasion. An example of this is found in Matthew 5–7. He asked questions (Matt. 16:13–20; John 21:15–17). He gave an example (Luke 11:1–4). He led discussions (Mark 10:17–45). He used the dramatic method (John 3:3–14). He employed the visual method (John 8:6).

I. THE IMPORTANCE OF METHOD

If method was important to Jesus, it should be to every teacher today. An old Sunday school proverb is, "Salt in the attic will not cure meat in the cellar." A teaching situation consists of a pupil, a teacher, and something to be taught and learned. The manner in which this something is taught will have much to do with the degree to which it is learned. The skill of the teacher in bringing together what is to be taught and the one who is to learn is vitally important.

Many Sunday school classes suffer from the routine of work "as usual." The teacher knows only one way to teach and he uses that way each Sunday. The class session is begun and concluded in the same manner. The few who respond to this method will learn, although a change in method would help them to learn more effectively. But there are some members who do not respond to this particular way of lesson presentation, so they find it more convenient to be absent than present.

The method should be varied not for the sake of being different but for the sake of arousing and maintaining interest so that real teaching may take place. In each instance the teacher should know why he is using certain methods and what he hopes to accomplish by doing so.

II. Factors in the Selection of Method

There are criteria which may serve to guide a teacher in selecting a method of teaching. These should be considered carefully before the teacher makes a final decision as to the method he plans to use.

1. *The Aim of the Teacher*

The purpose the teacher hopes to achieve will influence his choice of teaching methods. If it is to present the greatest amount of information in the lesson period, he may decide to lecture or make assignments for advance study and report in class. If he is trying to give a clearer interpretation of truth, he may use visual aids or tell a story. If his aim is primarily to stimulate the thinking of his members (and all teaching should stimulate thinking), he may decide to lead a discussion or raise a question.

Selecting a teaching aim should precede the choice of a method. In this manner the method used becomes a tool by which the teacher seeks to realize his aim. Otherwise it could become a device to suit the fancy of the teacher.

2. *The Nature of Lesson Materials*

The material to be taught influences the teacher's choice of a method. Some lessons, by their very nature, center around problems to be solved. They can be taught best by making the problem clear to all and leading a discussion which will help them discover a solution. There are other lessons which raise questions the answers to which may be brought out by a series of questions and answers. Some lessons are in story form, and others seem to invite a lecture. The nature and content of the printed lesson passage must be evaluated carefully before the teacher will have a conviction regarding the method which seems to fit the situation.

3. *The General Environment of Teaching*

There are hundreds of Sunday schools which have only one room in which to meet. Their only building is used for everything the church fosters—worship, teaching, and training. This means that several classes will be meeting in the auditorium simultaneously, often without the benefit of curtains or screens between the classes. This makes concentration necessary and real teaching difficult.

The one-room environment makes it difficult to vary the method of teaching. Often the teacher must do most of the talking to drown out other voices and keep attention. In a one-room building, teaching aids are at a premium. There is great need for chalkboards, maps, and charts, which are of great help in teaching. Many teachers have mastered these problems by securing movable partitions or screens with chalkboard space on one side and also space for hanging maps and charts. All of these environmental factors influence the choice and use of different methods of teaching.

4. *The Previous Experience and Maturity of the Pupils*

A teacher must know the background of his pupils in selecting teaching methods. In a college community where class members have a good educational background and are accustomed to assignments, discussions, questions, lectures, and the use of visual aids, the teacher will be able to employ all the methods at his command with more than average success.

If a teacher has a class of young people without such an educational background, but with a genuine interest in learning, he may find an immediate response to a variety of methods.

If, on the other hand, a teacher has a class which has been encouraged to be passive listeners by previous teachers in the Sunday school, he may find no interest or response at first to any method other than the lecture. Teaching by using other methods may prove rather discouraging for a while, but certainly the teacher should put forth every effort to get his members to respond to the various ways of presenting lesson truth.

5. *The Previous Experience and Skill of the Teacher*

Time is required to become skilful in the use of methods of teaching. When a teacher who has confined teaching to the use of one method learns of other methods, his usual procedure is to use one of the new methods the following Sunday. If he has been asking questions, he may decide to lead a discussion, which is one of the more difficult methods to use effectively. His members, taken by surprise, cannot adjust to the new procedure easily, so the teacher may decide not to use that method again.

He should realize that not being skilled in its use may prove discouraging both to him and the class. Perhaps the better plan would be to use the new method for only a part of the lesson period so that he and his members may get the "feel" of the new procedure. As this method is repeated, the teacher may become more and more efficient in its use.

The more skilled a teacher becomes, the less conscious he is of method. He almost instinctively makes his selection according to the needs to be met. In preparing to teach, he may plan to use a certain method or methods. But with practice he will find he can adjust to other methods of teaching as the need arises in the classroom. When he finishes the lesson period and reflects upon his teaching, he may be surprised at the number of methods he has used.

III. SOME METHODS OF TEACHING YOUNG PEOPLE

Without attempting an exhaustive discussion of all the methods of teaching, the remainder of this chapter will be devoted to a presentation of those methods which seem to meet the needs of young people best.

1. *The Discussion Method*

This method is devoted to problem solving. Since young people face so many problems, it has real significance for them. The discussion method consists of an interchange of individual opinions upon a problem, directed but not dominated by the teacher, so that all possible solutions to the problem are presented by the members, and usually a solution is reached which represents the best judgment of the group.

(1) *The necessity of a real problem.*—For this method to be successful, the discussion must center in a real problem. There must be differing points of view which will generate real interest. If all are agreed on the solution at the beginning, there will be practically no discussion. Therefore it is very important to have a clear statement of the problem so that all will understand it.

There must be a spirit of friendliness and fellowship in the class so that the members will be able to differ without becoming offended.

(2) *The vital role of the teacher.*—In the discussion the teacher plays a vital part. He must be tactful, patient, fair, tolerant, and poised. He must be mentally alert. He must know how to utilize different points of view. He must be able to analyze opinions accurately and discriminate between what will contribute to the discussion and what will not. If the discussion lags, he must know how to ask leading questions which introduce new life and interest. The teacher must maintain his control of the discussion without dominating it. When young people become interested in discussing a subject, their enthusiasm may take them away from the main problem to be solved. Each opinion must be welcomed even though temporarily it may have an adverse effect upon the discussion.

Sometimes, early in the discussion, members may ask the teacher to express his opinion. He should remember it is unwise for him to do so too soon. Many are willing to let others think for them. The purpose of the discussion is to train individuals to think for themselves and to contribute to the thinking of others. The teacher must not spend the class period trying to get the members to agree with him.

The teacher should call forth the best thinking in the class. He should know the subject well, and be ready with additional information if it is needed. A few pupils should not be allowed to monopolize the time. It is not the aim of the discussion method to have the members engage in idle discussion. All talk in the classroom should contribute to the solution of the problem.

Timid members should be encouraged to express themselves. Frequently the opinions of those who present them hesitantly are of the most value.

Many teachers have tried this method and have given it up in favor of the lecture, because they found it difficult to guide the discussion and arrive at worth-while conclusions. This is not due so much to the method as it is due to the teacher's lack of persistence in mastering it. The discussion should never become argumentation and debate. It should never degenerate into a presentation of prejudices.

(3) *The importance of preparation.*—Each member should be led to take the discussion seriously, and in so doing feel his responsibility for the use of the lesson period. This within itself will stimulate lesson preparation. The "give and take" of such procedure will teach each participant to speak cautiously so that he will not needlessly lay himself open to criticism.

The discussion will prove profitable only to the extent that the members make specific preparation before the lesson period. They must be stimulated to study the Bible, lesson helps, and other books and articles so that they may be prepared for their participation in the discussion. The teacher may prove helpful at this point by suggesting materials for study and research in advance of the discussion.

(4) *Testing the solution by Bible truths.*—There is always the problem that group thinking will not go far

enough in its decisions or that invalid conclusions will be reached. In order to prevent this, the teacher should have available certain references from the Bible to present to the class as guides in evaluating the concensus of their opinions as a discussion is concluded.

These standards of values and conduct will serve to evaluate the conclusions reached and direct individuals toward further thought and solution.

2. *The Question and Answer or Recitation Method*

To some, the name of this method may give a mental picture of a teacher calling upon the members one by one to answer questions. This method has been used in this manner in some classes. When the member answers his question, his responsibility is considered finished because he will not be asked another question. But this is not a correct interpretation of the question and answer method.

(1) *The values of questions.*—Stimulating thought questions are essential to good teaching. Perhaps too much teaching in the Sunday school has been directed toward answering questions in class rather than raising questions which would lead young people to study after the class period is over.

Questions may be used to find out what members know or do not know. They may help a person to interpret previous experience. A question may awaken curiosity and appeal to interest. It may direct thinking toward some significant topic. It gives an opportunity for a person to express himself. Questions often reveal the likes and dislikes of members and give the teacher an opportunity to provide the kind of information and guidance pupils need. By questioning, a teacher may review material taught previously and determine how well the members of the class learned it.

(2) *Difficulties in selecting good questions.*—Good

questions are not easily stated. Much practice is required in properly phrasing them. The teacher should practice this by writing out the leading thought questions which he plans to use during the lesson period. Evaluating these critically will do as much to improve the use of this method as anything else the teacher might do.

Effective questions should be brief. They should be stated simply and concisely. They should be clear and thought-provoking. They should not suggest the answers nor offer two possible answers. The questions should be logical and stimulating.

(3) *The techniques of questioning.*—When the teacher uses the question and answer method, he should attempt to keep the entire class interested. He may ask the question and glance over the entire class so as to encourage all the members to think of the answer. Sufficient time should be given for answering the question. It takes time to think. The inexperienced teacher dreads silence. If the answer is not immediately forthcoming, he will be tempted to answer his own question and go on to another. But he must not fall into this habit. If no one responds, he should call upon one of the members to answer the question. If the member called upon cannot answer, the teacher may ask another member to answer it. If no one can answer, he may ask the class to find the answer during the week.

As a rule, it is best not to repeat the question. If it is well phrased, one statement of it is sufficient. If it is poorly stated or misunderstood, it should be restated.

The teacher should avoid asking too many questions. They should not be of the yes and no type, but ones which challenge and invite serious thought. When asking questions, the teacher should use the conversational style of speaking.

(4) *Limitations of this method.*—This method has its

limitations. Merely asking questions is not teaching. The answer to a question is dependent upon previous knowledge and experience. Questions do not impart knowledge but help to open up new lines of thought. Of course, as answers to questions are shared in a class, those who do not know are taught by those who do.

Too often extremes in the use of this method are represented in the Sunday school. It is used too much or not at all. Perhaps its best use is in combination with other methods.

3. *The Lecture Method*

The teacher who lectures takes the major responsibility for the class session upon his own shoulders. The teacher, in preparing to teach, organizes his material in logical order. Then he uses the lesson period in telling the members what he knows about the lesson. Thus he is "in charge" for the entire time. The members of the class, knowing they are not to be called upon to participate in the discussion, make little if any preparation as a rule.

(1) *Advantages of the lecture method.*—But the lecture has its advantages as well as its disadvantages. It is not wholly bad. It is not simply "the passing of information from the notebook of the teacher to the notebook of the pupil without passing through the mind of either one," as someone has accused.

It appeals most to the mature mind; one which is trained to concentrate and follow logical, orderly procedure. The lecture offers full expression to the personality of the teacher. If the teacher is dynamic, lecturing gives this characteristic full play. If the teacher is dull, the lecture reveals this fact also. Thus the lecture is interesting if the lecturer is interesting. In the hands of the right person the lecture may become a means of arousing and motivating the members of the class.

The lecture economizes time. Since there is, at best, a teaching period of thirty-five or forty minutes in the Young People's class and there is quite a bit of biblical material to be covered, the teacher may feel that this may be done best if he uses all the time himself.

The teacher may feel that if he lectures, he can give a better summary of the material and also bring in supplementary material which is not known to the pupils. In this way, because of the greater knowledge and experience of the teacher, the class will actually have access to knowledge which they would not have otherwise.

(2) *Disadvantages of the lecture method.*—However, there are distinct disadvantages in the use of the lecture.

It enlists only a minimum of participation. Unless other methods of teaching are used in connection with it, and unless the teacher is gifted in the use of the lecture, there will be comparatively little thinking and response in the class.

If one uses this method exclusively, it will cut down on the pupil's actual contact with the Bible itself. Knowing that the teacher will tell him about the lesson truth, the pupil is inclined to let him do his work for him. Thus he does not put forth the effort to learn for himself which is essential if learning takes place. In colleges and universities where the lecture method is used the most, it is always used in connection with assignments. The students are studying outside the class and taking notes on the lectures in the classroom. In other words, the lecture is supplemented with activities to secure pupil participation and activity.

The use of this method requires skill in public speaking. Being able to express oneself forcefully and clearly is essential to success. This explains why some classes become crystallized around a teacher. Young people do not want to leave a teacher who is a forceful lecturer, because there may not be another personality as outstanding to become the teacher of another class. Such a teacher should be quick to sense this problem. He should realize that one of his greatest contributions could be made in leading the members of his class to reorganize into several smaller classes where better teaching would result. Other teachers not as skilled in the use of the lecture could be enlisted to teach the new classes, and more actual learning could take place.

The large class often appeals to the vanity of the teacher. Without being conscious of this fact, he desires to keep it large in order to satisfy his own sense of importance. In doing so he not only hinders the enlistment of other young people, but hinders the learning opportunities of the ones he has.

Teachers who use the lecture method tend to use it to excess. Sometimes it becomes the chief competitor of the morning worship service. Two sermons regularly each Sunday will inevitably compete with each other. If class members participate in a well-planned lesson, they are more likely to attend the morning worship service.

In order to be successful in lecturing, the teacher must secure and keep the attention of the class. He must seek to get the members to remember what he has said. They must be convinced of the truth of the lecture and be given direction in carrying out the decisions which they make.

4. *The Story Method*

The story is a method of teaching which has universal interest and appeal. Seldom will it be used as the method for an entire lesson period in the Young People's class. But it has uses which make it distinctive. Its values should be understood by all teachers of this age group. Every great teacher and preacher is effective in the use of the story.

(1) *Some values of the story.*—There are many reasons why the story is valuable. Stories stir the imagination and appeal to action. They secure interest and attention because they are dramatic. Clearly told, stories make truth more vivid than most methods of teaching. After the telling of a story the member grasps the truth for himself without further exhortation from the teacher.

Stories are often remembered after the lesson has been concluded in the classroom. When they are recalled, the truth which they convey is further impressed.

Stories serve to make members ready for additional learning opportunities. They add variety and life to discussions.

If stories are overused, they may become monotonous as any other method would with constant use. Young people who have learned to deal with ideas and logical procedures of thought will not be challenged by an overuse of stories. Many associate this method with the children's classes of the Sunday school, where it is one of the principal methods of teaching.

(2) *Selecting a story to meet a need.*—In using a story, the teacher should have a genuine need for doing so. Of course, if the lesson itself is a Bible story, this fact may cause the teacher to select the story method for conveying the truth. But this will not occur often in a lesson series.

When the story is used for only a part of the lesson period, the teacher should search for a story to meet the need or even create a story for the purpose.

In making his selection, the teacher should choose a story on the level of the understanding and appreciation of the class. In presenting it, he must not "talk down" to his members but tell the story in language which they will appreciate because of its evident maturity.

(3) *The importance of study and practice.*—Contrary to the beliefs of many, not everyone presents a story well.

Much study is required if a story is presented properly. The teacher must read and reread it until he has an appreciation of the story as a whole. As his study continues, the scenes should stand out clearly in his mind. The characters should live and the narrative should become real to him. The events should take a logical sequence in the teacher's thinking and lead to the climax of the story.

The teacher should practice telling the story. This will make it clearer to him, relieve him of self-consciousness, and give him poise and self-confidence.

When he tells the story to his class, he should be unaffected. He should not be too concerned about gestures, using only those which will help convey greater meaning to his hearers. As far as possible, he will forget himself and concentrate upon the story. It should be an experience which he is sharing with his hearers. The story should be permitted to carry its own lesson. The teacher should make every effort to make his hearers feel this lesson which the story has for them.

(4) *Ways of using stories.*—There are various ways in which the story may be used for teaching young people. As previously indicated, it may be used as the method for teaching the entire lesson. This will be done only occasionally.

A story may be used in connection with other methods. It may serve to introduce the lesson. A well-told story may begin a lecture, a discussion, or a question and answer period in the class. It may be used to illustrate a truth or make the meaning clear. It may offer the solution to a problem which has been discussed. It may be used at the close of a lesson period to motivate to action.

5. *The Combination Method*

Although different methods of teaching have been discussed, it is almost impossible to put these different methods into airtight compartments. Teaching is usually done best when a combination of methods is followed.

(1) *Combination inevitable.*—From a careful study of almost any lesson period, the teacher will find that more than one method of teaching was used.

A teacher may begin a lesson by using the question and answer method. But the question may awaken such an interest the rest of the period may be spent in group discussion. In lecturing, the teacher may tell a story and then find the remainder of the period is spent in problem solving.

(2) *Combination not a matter of chance.*—The combination of methods, however, should never be left to chance nor to the impulse of the moment. It is well for the teacher to think through the possible class procedure, then select the methods which fit his aim for the lesson.

When occasions arise in the lesson period requiring a change in methods, the teacher should do his best to make choices wisely. He should select the method which seems to be the best for meeting the needs of the situation. This departure from the original plan should continue only long enough to meet these needs. Following this, the teacher should return to his original plan.

The teacher is not expected to give ready-made solutions to life problems. He is a fellow learner with his pupils. If the teacher sets out to establish a spirit of freedom and informality, encouraging the members to participate in the lesson period, young people will hold their teacher in admiration and look forward to their class session with joy.

The best way to become proficient in teaching is to observe how people learn when they are not in school. In the truest sense they learn from living. Speaking in general terms the one best method of teaching is the one which life offers. If the teacher can offer opportunities for actually doing what he is trying to teach, learning will be far more effective.

IV. VISUAL AIDS IN TEACHING

There is a new appreciation of the use of visual aids in teaching. Many books and magazine articles are appearing which offer assistance to the teacher in understanding their values and use. This brief discussion regarding them should be supplemented by further study.

1. *Values in Visual Aids*

Visual aids have many values in teaching. They add pleasure to learning. They are not for entertainment, but their use does make learning more enjoyable. They also accelerate learning. Excellent results were achieved with visual aids in the training program of the armed forces during World War II.

When visual aids are used, much of what one learns is remembered. They also enrich the content of learning. A vast field of new materials opens when one begins using visual aids. They motivate action. Picturing a desirable trait clearly will often stimulate a person to seek an outlet of expression for the truth he has learned.

2. *Principles in Using Visual Aids*

The proper educational principles should be followed in using visual aids. Their use should be based upon actual need. A teacher who uses visual aids just to be using them often will waste his time and the time of the class in doing so. When some aid is used, it should be selected because it will meet the purpose of the teacher better than anything else. It should be used in connection with regular materials and activities. It is not a substitute for regular Bible study but should be chosen to make Bible study more vital and attractive.

Visual aids should be chosen and used according to accepted learning procedures. They must be interesting and in keeping with the needs of the class members. They should also be within the range of the pupil's understanding and appreciation. They should direct attention and interest toward what the pupils need to know and appreciate.

3. Nonprojected Visual Aids

There are many visual aids which are usable in teaching young people. For a full discussion each teacher should read carefully *Teaching and Training with Audio-Visuals* by Earl Waldrup, published by the Convention Press, Nashville, Tennessee. Only a brief discussion of the available aids will be attempted here.

(1) *The chalkboard.*—One of the best of all visual aids is the chalkboard. Chalkboards may be movable or attached to the wall. They should be considered standard equipment for every Young People's classroom. Many churches do provide them for the teachers' use. But some teachers who have chalkboards in their classrooms do not use them.

Each teacher should plan in advance how he will use the board. He may write his outline there before the lesson begins. He may write it there as the lesson develops. He may write unfamiliar words or sketch diagrams as his needs require.

(2) *Flat pictures.*—The values of flat pictures are well known. They arouse interest, give reality to lesson truth, give information, stimulate group discussion and further study. For a long time most Sunday school workers believed pictures could be used with children only. But if the pictures are in the areas of their interest, young peo-

ple will respond to their use as will any other age group.

There is much to commend the use of flat pictures. They are cheap and abundant. The teacher may cut out, mount, and use his own pictures at low cost. Often the covers of his lesson helps may be used to good effect. All pictures should be large enough to be seen by all and should be used when they meet a real need in the class.

(3) *Maps, posters, and charts.*—Maps, posters, and charts are valuable visual aids. Each class should have its own map or maps for use in Bible study. If it is not possible to purchase them, some young person might be asked to sketch one on the board or heavy paper for use. Travel agencies, many magazines, and newspapers publish maps which may be collected and used.

Posters are designed to catch the attention of individuals and hold it long enough to impress a truth vividly upon their minds. No doubt young people with talent in poster making could be enlisted to prepare posters to make the truth of certain lessons striking and penetrating.

Charts showing the progress of the class, the delinquency of youth, or any other vital subject might be prepared by a member for use in class. The chart is used to arrange data for study and comparison. Such an aid may be used at times by the teacher.

(4) *Objects and models.*—Certain objects and models may prove helpful in teaching. This type of visual aid may prove especially useful in educating the class in missions. Objects from some country will bring the customs and needs of the people before the members better than almost any other media. If a church has a place where such objects may be kept for use, so much the better.

(5) *The field trip.*—The field trip is an excellent aid in teaching. This involves a visit by the class to some place where they may observe situations and experiences for

themselves. Seeing at first hand the work, living conditions, and need of others will create much more interest and understanding than simply discussing the subject in class.

4. *Projected Visual Aids*

The use of projected aids in the classroom has been limited by lack of space, equipment, and finances. Slides, filmstrips, films, and projectors are expensive. If used in classes, much equipment will be required.

Projected aids have been used mostly in general and department assemblies. More use should be made of these aids. If there are separate classrooms of sufficient size, with electrical outlets, the teacher may be able to secure a projector and visual materials for use. Present-day equipment, which makes it possible to use projected aids without darkening the room, makes possible an effective use of such materials in teaching. An increasing number of churches are investing in equipment and materials for use by Sunday school teachers. Often teachers and class members take pictures with their own cameras which they may use in connection with the course of study. The teacher should capitalize upon all such opportunities.

FOR FURTHER STUDY

1. Of the methods discussed, which is the most difficult for you to use? What can you do to improve in the use of this method?
2. From your study of next Sunday's lesson, which method, or methods, would you select for teaching it? Why?
3. What visual aids are available for your use? What visual aids would be most useful in teaching next Sunday's lesson?
4. Suggest that various methods of teaching be demonstrated frequently in the officers and teachers' meeting.
6. Examine the teaching suggestions in your current copy of *The Young People's Teacher* and mark the various methods suggested by the lesson writer in the procedure outlined in the lessons for the month.

CHAPTER 6

I. FORMING WORTHY STUDY HABITS

1. A Regular Time and Place
2. Begin Early
3. Study Widely
4. Consider Class Members

II. USING AVAILABLE SOURCES

1. Lesson Helps
2. A Personal Library
3. Newspaper and Magazine Materials

III. MAKING TOTAL PREPARATION

1. Prepare Physically
2. Prepare Socially
3. Prepare Spiritually

IV. WORKING OUT A TEACHING PLAN

1. Begin with Prayer
2. Concentrate upon the Lesson Passage
3. Recall the Interests and Needs of the Members
4. Select an Aim
5. Plan the Introduction
6. Plan for Participation
7. Relate the Lesson to Life
8. Awaken Interest in the Next Lesson
9. Evaluate the Plan

6

The Teacher Preparing to Teach

Study to shew thyself approved unto God
(2 Tim. 2:15)

TEACHING will be a rich and rewarding experience if the teacher is prepared. If his preparation is inadequate, the class session will become dull, drab, and colorless. Each teacher must pay the price of preparation if he succeeds with his class.

I. FORMING WORTHY STUDY HABITS

Spasmodic preparation will not prove satisfactory. Regular study, if possible day after day, is the answer to a teacher's study needs.

1. *A Regular Time and Place*

Each teacher should plan his time so that he may study each day. No person *has* time for all he is called on to do. He must *take* time for what is most essential. One of the principal problems of the beginning teacher is the readjustment of his schedule so that he may have some study time each day. Maintaining a regular time schedule is difficult even for the experienced teacher.

The best time for study varies with each teacher. Some teachers study early in the morning, others late at night, and the rest at times between these extremes. Few people will have long periods of time for concentrated study. One's day is divided into minute portions so he will have to make the most of the time at his disposal. Lesson preparation should not be postponed until late in the week. The effectiveness of teaching is lost by this habit.

Not only should there be a regular time for study each day, there should also be a regular place for study. These two factors will help a teacher to concentrate upon his work better than most other habits of study he may form.

The place for study should be a desk or table where books and study materials are within reach of the teacher. This will encourage study more than having to gather up books and materials and take them to a special place. A comfortable straight chair is the best type of chair to use. The place of study should afford good lighting, proper ventilation, and quietude. Coming to the same place at the same time each day will have much to do with getting effective study done.

2. *Begin Early*

The preceding statement may suggest to some that preparation should begin on Sunday afternoon. If at all possible, the specific preparation of the next Sunday's lesson should begin by that time. But over-all preparation should have begun before then.

Well before the beginning of a new quarter, the teacher should preview the lessons for that quarter. If the school offers a preview study, the teacher should participate. Guidance material for the preview study of a given quarter's lessons is offered in *The Young People's Teacher* for the last month of the preceding quarter. Credit in the Church Study Course, category 17, section for Adults and Young People, may be received for such study. Individuals may gain much from using the preview guidance material in home study.

Each teacher should begin the quarter by planning to teach the entire series of lessons as a unit. Although he is to teach a lesson at a time, he should plan to teach each one in relation to the others. This will give coherence and emphasis to his teaching.

After making such inclusive preparation, the teacher will be ready to concentrate upon his study week by week. But if this study is made only a week in advance, much of the effectiveness of lesson preparation will be lost. If he is to make assignments and enlist his members in study outside the class, the teacher will have to make some preparation at least two weeks in advance. In doing so he can make assignments on one Sunday for the following Sunday's lesson. Preparing for two or three weeks in advance will add zest and interest to his teaching.

3. *Study Widely*

The teacher should study more of the Bible than the lesson series. Only by additional study will his teaching be enriched.

He should take advantage of the study opportunities offered him by his church. He should take the books taught in training courses and during the January Bible Study Week. He should enrol at each opportunity, buy a book, study carefully, and attend each class period.

In addition, he should plan a personal program of Bible reading and study. He should read the Bible through as often as possible. He could read many of the shorter books of the Bible at one sitting, making notes on passages to look up in a Bible commentary for more careful study.

He may desire to study the Bible biographically or topically. As he does so, he may make notations in his Bible or in a notebook, where he would have the information when it is needed later.

Although each teacher must major on the study of the Bible itself, he should study as many books as possible about the Bible. General training course books which are of great value to the teacher are listed in category 2 of the Church Study Course. The Bible Survey Plan will lead to a reasonably thorough acquaintance with the Bible as a whole. Books on Bible geography and customs, and books of exposition, are listed in the *Baptist Book Store Catalog*.

Each teacher should read denominational magazines and papers. Often an exposition of the Sunday school lessons appears in the state Baptist paper. Articles of general interest give the teacher information he should know. Many illustrations will come from *The Commission* and *Home Missions*.

As far as possible the teacher should read current magazines. The wider the range of interest, the more he will be able to influence young people. As a teacher discovers the interests of his class members, he may read in their fields of interest. This will assist him in discussing matters of importance to them.

Often many illustrations and much helpful information will come from the daily newspapers. The sections read most widely by young people are the comics, the athletic section, and the society pages. Reading these sections often gives points of contact not otherwise open to the teacher.

Current books should be on the teacher's list also. He need not attempt to read all the "best sellers." However, many books of fiction are based upon the Bible. Young people read these and raise questions regarding them. The teacher will find it profitable to read them and will need to know where fact ends and fiction begins in such books. The best of these books will stimulate his own thought.

4. Consider Class Members

It is important to study the Bible. But a successful teacher must know the needs of each class member also. When the teacher is preparing to teach, the class roll and

Bible should be on the study desk together. The truth of the Bible is needed by each member of the class. But he will not receive this truth unless the teacher plans to make it interesting and desirable to him.

This fact indicates that a class of young people should not have a large enrolment. No teacher can teach as he should if he does not know and understand each member well. A large enrolment does not encourage such understanding.

By visiting the members during the week, the teacher will become better acquainted with them. When lesson study begins, he will draw upon this information as a part of his preparation for teaching the lesson.

This discussion on preparation should not discourage those who have a limited time to give to it. Preparation for teaching is going on much of the time. The experiences one has offer possibilities for illustrations. General reading and contacts afford information to the person who keeps his lesson in mind during the week. It is hoped that this discussion will challenge each teacher to use the time he has to the best advantage and to appear before his class each Sunday after having made full preparation.

II. Using Available Sources

The teacher is not lacking in excellent materials as he seeks to prepare himself for effective teaching.

1. *Lesson Helps*

The Sunday School Board, through its editorial service, provides excellent materials for the teacher. Beginning in October, 1956, the Board has prepared *The Young People's Teacher,* a monthly periodical with specialized helps for teachers of married Young People, and for those who teach single Young People. It carries the Uniform Lesson text with Scripture references covering the background material. This is followed by an exposition for the teacher's personal study and suggestions for teaching the lesson to meet the specific needs of the various groups of young people. From this rich store the teacher will select what is best for his own class, adding further material from his wider study.

The Young People's Teacher is his best help. It is prepared by Baptists for Baptists. It is Bible-based, rich in content, doctrinally sound, and it follows sound educational principles. Every teacher may use it with confidence.

In addition to *The Young People's Teacher,* each teacher should have a copy of the quarterly used by his own class members—either *Sunday School Young People* or *Sunday School Married Young People*. This will provide the teacher with all the lessons under one cover, in one piece of literature. It will enable the teacher to become familiar with the suggestions for study offered his members, and to use their lesson preparation in his teaching.

Copies of *The Young People's Teacher* and either *Sunday School Young People* or *Sunday School Married Young People* should be ordered by the church for all teachers of young people. Each young person should receive from the church a copy of his study help each quarter.

The Sunday School Builder offers additional help to each teacher through the general articles, the section on Young People's work, the suggestions for the teaching improvement periods, and the lesson expositions.

These lesson helps are the best investment a church can make, providing teachers and class members are led to show their appreciation by using them in regular Bible study.

In addition to the lesson periodicals, the Sunday School Board publishes *Broadman Comments* annually. This is a book offering additional helpful material for those who teach the Uniform Series. *Points for Emphasis* is a concise, pocket-size lesson help which many teachers find handy and useful.

One great advantage in having the lesson helps in book form is that it provides the lesson outlines and discussions over the span of an entire year. In this way a teacher may look beyond a current quarter's lessons and know something of what he is to teach in coming months. Additional suggestions and outlines are included in the book. These enrich the teacher's preparation for his task.

2. *A Personal Library*

Every teacher should make some effort toward building a library of tools for his work. There is more involved in this than buying books. One can buy many books and still not have what he needs. Books are expensive, and each teacher should be certain that each book he buys is usable and valuable to him.

There are basic books which each teacher needs. He should have more than one version of the Bible. The King James Version is basic. Another version for reading and study will prove helpful. Other valuable books will be: a one-volume Bible commentary, a Bible dictionary, a concordance, and a Bible atlas. There are excellent books in these classifications. One's pastor or minister of religious education can offer helpful suggestions regarding the purchase of books. The Baptist Book Store serving each state will be able to make good recommendations also.

More and more churches are providing books for the use of their teachers through church libraries. This is one of the best investments which any church can make in the improvement of teaching. When the church provides such opportunities, each teacher should use these books as they are needed.

3. Newspaper and Magazine Materials

A further step in preparing to teach may be taken by those who are willing to invest extra time. Building a file of helpful material is one of the best means of being prepared. The teacher may build a file classified according to general topics. If he builds it just for the teaching of a particular series, he may develop it around the subjects of the lessons he is to teach. By looking ahead he becomes familiar with the subjects of forthcoming lessons. He may secure thirteen envelopes for the next quarter's series and write the subject of each lesson. As he reads, he may clip information which he thinks he can use and file it in the proper envelope. When he is ready to make specific preparation of that lesson, he will already have excellent material to use. He will no doubt have more information in some envelopes than he will be able to use. All material which is not used may then be filed topically so that he may draw upon it for future use. In this way each teacher builds up a reservoir of information which he will be using as he needs it.

III. MAKING TOTAL PREPARATION

There is more to preparation than the preparing of one's mind.

1. Prepare Physically

Leading people requires a great amount of physical and nervous energy. Late hours on Saturday night often ruin the mental preparation which the teacher has made. The Jewish sabbath began at sundown on the preceding day. This enabled the worshipers to be rested and ready for their experiences with God on the day of worship. Can a Christian afford to do less than this if it is possible for him to have his Saturday evening free? If one accepts social engagements on Saturday evening which deprive him of rest, he may sleep late on Sunday morning, rush away to his responsibilities nervous and irritable, only to feel that he has failed in his work that day. The pessimism of Elijah left him after he rested and the Lord fed him (1 Kings 19).

Each teacher should look his best when he meets with his class for Bible study. He should be clean, neat, and as attractive as his circumstances permit. He should look good and smell good. Perhaps the Baptist Book Stores will feature a perfume someday made especially for Sunday school workers.

2. *Prepare Socially*

Sunday school attendance is not compulsory. Young people attend because they desire to do so. A fine, wholesome spirit on the part of the teacher will have much to do with encouraging regular attendance. A complaining, criticizing, faultfinding teacher will never build a class of young people. "He that thinketh by the inch and complaineth by the yard ought to be kicked by the foot."

3. *Prepare Spiritually*

The most important phase of preparation is the spiritual. After making the best mental, physical, and social preparation, each teacher should place himself at the disposal of the Holy Spirit. No one should approach so holy a task as the interpretation of the truth of God's Word without complete dedication to the will and purpose of God. The best workman is the one who has learned how to work with God. Christ said, "I am the vine, ye are the branches: He that abideth in me, and I in him, the same bringeth forth much fruit: for without me ye can do nothing" (John 15:5).

IV. Working Out a Teaching Plan

The specific preparation of the teacher should result in a well worked out plan for teaching. This will seem difficult to those who have never tried it. But if each teacher will begin working along definite lines in lesson preparation, he will find greater satisfaction and security in such preparation.

1. *Begin with Prayer*

Each teacher should begin his preparation with prayer and dedication to the will of God. This should not become a meaningless form but should be a time of spiritual commitment to the leadership of the Holy Spirit. Teaching is a service in obedience to the command of Christ. In handling the Bible to meet the spiritual needs of members one will need divine wisdom and guidance from the beginning of his preparation. Without hesitation one should ask God for this leadership as he begins his preparation.

2. *Concentrate upon the Lesson Passage*

This is the time to make specific preparation of the printed passage. Finding the reference in the lesson helps, one should then locate the passage in his Bible and read and reread it there. Before reading the comments of lesson writers, one should find out first of all what is revealed to him through his own reading of the lesson passage.

As he reflects upon the Scripture passage, he should write down the thoughts and questions which come to his mind. These will not be in logical form or sequence as a rule but can be organized into such an arrangement later. He should note unfamiliar words and phrases which he will look up in his Bible dictionary or commentary.

This may be as much as the teacher can accomplish during his first study period. But understanding the lesson passage at the beginning of his preparation will set his mind to work upon it. Around its truths he will find that ideas and experiences will cluster during the week.

3. *Recall the Interests and Needs of the Members*

Another step in lesson preparation will be the study of the class roll. Having become familiar with the lesson passage, the teacher should go over his class roll name by name, trying to discover areas of need which the lesson will meet.

His aim in preparation should not be to impress the class members with how much he knows, but to be able to use what he knows in meeting the needs of these members.

He will draw upon his knowledge of his members at this point in his preparation. If he is in close contact with them, he will have an abundance of material for use. If he lacks information regarding his members, perhaps this part of preparation should be spent in visiting them to secure the information needed.

4. *Select an Aim*

With knowledge of the lesson passage and of the needs of class members, one is ready to select an aim for teaching. Each teacher will attempt to put into a sentence or two what he hopes to accomplish by the teaching of the lesson. This will be slow and tedious for most teachers. Yet it is one of the most important steps in developing a teaching plan. It is important for the teacher to know what he is to teach, whom he is to teach, and why he is teaching. The statement of the aim is in answer to the question, "Why?" He might begin his aim in these words,

"To lead my class members to . . ." or "To guide the members of my class to . . ." or some similar statement. Comparing and discussing these predetermined aims at the weekly officers and teachers' meeting will be a helpful process.

5. *Plan the Introduction*

Introducing the lesson is very important. The lesson must begin where the pupils are. It must tie in with their interests and needs so as to capture their attention.

The teacher should spend whatever amount of time is needed in choosing the proper way to begin the lesson. It must be planned in keeping with the content and aim of the lesson as well as the needs of the members.

Some introductions are too interesting. If one begins his lesson with last Saturday's football game, he may never bring his discussion around to the lesson for the day.

Some introductions are too dull. A teacher had the habit of beginning each lesson with the question, "What is our lesson about today?" One Sunday there was a visitor in his class. That morning the teacher began by asking his customary question, "What is our lesson about to-day?" As usual, he got no response though he repeated it twice. After the third time, the visitor reached for his hat and said, "If the teacher doesn't know, I'm going home."

The teacher may find a question, a story, a picture, a chalkboard outline, a letter, the reading of a Scripture passage, or some other way will give him the start he needs in teaching the lesson.

How to introduce a lesson is also a good topic to discuss at the weekly officers and teachers' meeting.

6. *Plan for Participation*

At this stage of his preparation the teacher should re-mind himself that he must do everything possible to get his members to take part in the learning process. He wants them to think, evaluate, analyze, discuss, ask questions, and share what they know and have experienced with the class. He will not plan to do their thinking for them but to get them to think constructively for themselves.

The aim for the lesson should be written out where the teacher can keep it in view. As he considers it, he will think of the procedures to follow in accomplishing that aim. Shall he lecture, raise a problem and lead the class to discuss it, formulate some stimulating questions, or choose a combination of methods?

When the teacher answers this question, he will proceed to develop his plan. If he lectures, the use of the chalkboard, pictures, and the Bible will be some activities which will further the learning process. If he uses the discussion method, he must define the problem, think of possible solutions, and determine ways of guiding the discussion.

Should the question and answer method be selected, the teacher must formulate a few key questions and think of the possible ways in which they will be answered. He must also try to prepare for the questions which members of the class will raise.

If illustrations are to be used, the teacher must seek for those which will meet the needs of this session of the class. If he has been building a file for this purpose, it will be a fruitful source for his use at this time.

One of the best ways of securing participation is to make assignments before the class meets. This is true especially if one's class is unaccustomed to participating in the lesson period.

The teacher should go over the assignment with the member, pointing out the difficulties involved in carrying it out, and showing its relationship to the lesson and the quarter's lessons. The proper instructions should be given for carrying out the assignment. References in the Bible, Bible commentaries, and other books should be provided. The teacher should indicate at what time the member is to present his information during the lesson period. The assignments should not be made in the classroom, but if possible during visits in the homes of the young people.

7. *Relate the Lesson to Life*

Because this is discussed as a later step in lesson preparation, it does not follow that only the last few minutes of each lesson must be devoted to showing where the lesson has significance for each member. All of the lesson should apply, and it should be making its application as it is taught. If the lesson begins with the interests and needs of the members, if they are led to participate in the lesson study, and if the class session is meaningful to them, they will make their own application. The teacher has not taught unless they do. Thus the objective of the teacher is to get them to do something about the truth they learn.

8. *Awaken Interest in the Next Lesson*

Preparation for teaching is not over until the teacher has turned his attention to the lesson for the following Sunday. He should plan to get his members to prepare it and be ready to take part in the study on next Sunday. By showing possibilities for learning new truth, the teacher may get his pupils to study more.

He should plan to announce the subject of the lesson, refer to the Bible passage, tell an interesting incident which will introduce the central truth, or choose some other way to awaken interest in the next lesson.

9. *Evaluate the Plan*

When the plan is complete, the teacher should look it over with a critical eye. Is the aim adequate? Will the introduction secure interest and attention? Will the methods which have been selected serve to help the teacher reach his aim? Has he planned to secure the participation of the class members? Has the lesson for the following Sunday become sufficiently clear to him so that he may make it clear to others?

Each teacher should be his own best critic. He should be seeking constantly to find better ways of presenting the Bible truth.

FOR FURTHER STUDY

1. What lesson helps do you use: *The Young People's Teacher, Broadman Comments,* a Bible dictionary, a concordance, an atlas? If these lesson helps are not available, suggest they be placed in your church library for use.
2. Do you make mental, physical, social, and spiritual preparation for teaching? In which of these is your preparation the poorest? What can you do to improve at this point?
3. Take the suggested outline in the chapter on making a teaching plan and use it in preparing to teach the lesson for next Sunday. Which step seems the most difficult for you? Remember, "Practice makes perfect."
4. Take your outline to the weekly officers and teachers' meeting and ask the opinions of your fellow workers regarding it.

CHAPTER 7

I. SETTING THE STAGE FOR TEACHING
   1. The Classroom and Its Equipment
   2. The Arrangement of the Room
   3. The Significance of the Assembly Period
   4. The Beginning of the Class Session

II. CREATING A SPIRIT OF FRIENDLINESS AND FREEDOM

   1. The Importance of Atmosphere
   2. The Teacher's Part

III. SECURING ATTENTION AND INTEREST

   1. Begin with Something Vital
   2. Guide Attention into Sustained Interest
   3. Procedure Subject to Change

IV. GETTING PARTICIPATION

   1. Call for Assignments
   2. Use the Bible
   3. Encourage Questions
   4. Direct Discussion
   5. Watch the Time

V. ARRIVING AT WORTHWHILE CONCLUSIONS

   1. Remembering the Aim
   2. Testing Conclusions with Bible Truth
   3. An Example from the Teaching of Jesus

VI. STIMULATING FURTHER LEARNING

   1. "Closing" Each Lesson Unnecessary
   2. Capitalizing upon Pupil Interest

7

The Teacher Teaching Effectively

For he taught them as one having authority
(Matt. 7:29)

EVERY LESSON is more impressive if a proper background has been created for it. Each teacher should take the initiative in seeing that this is done.

I. SETTING THE STAGE FOR TEACHING

The environment of teaching has much to do with the success of the learning process. That is the principal reason why churches are investing their funds in educational buildings.

1. *The Classroom and Its Equipment*

In providing educational space, attention should be given to the Young People's classroom and equipment. The room should be located adjacent to the department assembly room. It should be decorated in an attractive color, or colors. The windows should have blinds, shades, or draperies. If possible, there should be a floor covering of some kind. Many of the newer buildings have asphalt tile on the floors. This makes them more attractive and easy to keep. The room should be well lighted and ventilated. There should be a table for the teacher and a table for the secretary.

At the front of the room there should be a chalkboard and space for charts, maps, and posters. One or two well-chosen pictures should be hung on the walls, at the eye level of the members. When they are placed there, the teacher should interpret their meaning to the members so that their message will be repeated each time the members see them.

Many churches cannot have space and equipment of this kind. If all the classes must meet in a one-room building, the young people's teacher will seek to make teaching conditions as favorable as possible. He may take the lead in providing curtains, movable partitions, and such other equipment as the church may be able to secure. In making any plans of this nature, he should first carry his plans to the pastor and general superintendent. The church should provide the equipment rather than the teachers and classes.

2. The Arrangement of the Room

Often teachers with the best equipment do not make use of it. Where the class has a separate room, attention should be given to preparing it for the lesson period. The teacher should arrive from fifteen to thirty minutes before time for the assembly program to begin. He may ask various members of the class to meet him at that time to give special attention to arranging the room.

It is assumed the room has been swept and dusted. However, in many churches dust is found on the chairs when members enter their classrooms. This raises questions about janitor service, but Sunday morning is not a good time to settle these. The chairs must be dusted and, if this is not done before the class session, it will take time from the lesson period to do it after the class assembles. The teacher and class members should not have to do this regularly, but there will be emergencies of this nature to be met.

The room should be given proper ventilation. The chalk and eraser should be in place. The chairs should be arranged informally. The secretary's table should be at the back of the room, and the teacher's table at the front. Equipment is often moved out of the room during the week and does not find its way back as often as it is moved.

Young women will take pleasure in arranging flowers for their room. If one arrangement is placed at the front of the room, it will help to focus attention there.

3. The Significance of the Assembly Period

One of the best ways to prepare young people for lesson study is to lead them to attend the assembly period.

Young people come on Sunday morning with their minds filled with the events of the week. Activities of school, business, and home are uppermost in their thinking. Sunday dinners and afternoon trips have been planned following the morning services. The teacher's competition is keen. Something must be done to get the class members to push these experiences into the background and prepare their minds for the reception of spiritual truth.

The assembly program is the real answer to this need. Participating in singing, praying, Scripture reading, and the other elements of the service will lead the members into fellowship with God. When this is done, the experiences of the week will not seem so significant. Pupils will be more receptive of the truth. Participation will unify thinking and guide them in becoming fellow learners.

4. The Beginning of the Class Session

The spirit created in the assembly period should be carried over into the class session. The president of the class will have much to do in making this possible. He should take charge of the class as it assembles. The class session should begin with prayer. Following this the president will call upon the vice-president, who will recognize the presence of any visitors or prospective members. If some members have returned after an extended absence, mention should be made of this fact. He will ask the group leaders to make reports of interest to the class.

Under the leadership of the president the reports on the Six Point Record System will be secured from those who are present. This part of the class period should never be permitted to become the business session of the class. The weekly or monthly business meeting of the class officers is for this purpose. The work of the class officers and members is a part of the total teaching program of the class. Those who render service have many opportunities for learning through such activities. Participation in the program of the class during the week and on Sundays will develop an interest nothing else can do.

II. CREATING A SPIRIT OF FRIENDLINESS AND FREEDOM

If there is an interchange of information and experience in the classroom, a spirit of freedom must be created which will encourage it.

1. *The Importance of Atmosphere*

The importance of pupil participation in learning has been discussed previously. Even when the value of getting the members to take part is known, it is not easy to lead them to do so. There will be little if any response unless the pupils are in an atmosphere where it is easy for them to take part.

This does not mean that young people must be permitted to "take over" the class period. With a limited teaching period at best, genuine learning could never result by giving free rein to the impulses of a group of young people.

But they must be led to feel they are under the guidance of their best friend, their teacher. They must feel they are more important to him than his lesson outline. They must be sure that he wants to help them solve their problems, give them spiritual truth, and help them to achieve their cherished goals in life more than anything else.

In that sense, then, they are free to raise questions, ask for additional information, confess they are confused and bewildered, and indicate their need for closer contact with God.

2. *The Teacher's Part*

The spirit the teacher brings into the classroom with him will have much to do with the attitude of the members of the class. If the teacher has prepared to include his pupils in the lesson study, this fact will become known very quickly. If his goal is to make them active rather than passive, they will sense this and feel free in his presence.

If his teaching has a sense of mission, it will seem only logical for the members to push personal whims and fancies into the background and use the time to achieve some worth-while goals for themselves.

To further the spirit of freedom, the teacher may take a few moments to express appreciation for the effective work of the officers and members at the beginning of the lesson period. He may indicate his pleasure over the attendance of the class. If some of the pupils asked questions about the lesson after class on the preceding Sunday, the teacher may commend them for doing so without calling their names. There are many ways of exhibiting friendliness without saying, "I am your friend" or "I love young people."

The teacher will not do the same things each week, but

he must let the class members know that the lesson period is for them and that he is there to join them in the adventure of learning. If he makes clear he appreciates their participation, he will get it, even though it may take a long while to accomplish this goal.

If a teacher will employ a conversational tone of voice in teaching, this will secure greater freedom in the class. Some teachers find it more informal to be seated while they teach, although this would not suit every teacher. Each teacher will work for informality, but should not "let down the bars," permitting young people to discuss anything they like or do anything they desire to do. They are in the class for Bible study. The teacher should never forget this.

III. Securing Attention and Interest

It is not possible to teach unless the teacher has the attention and interest of his pupils.

1. *Begin with Something Vital*

The way in which the lesson begins has much to do with its success. If the beginning is not interesting, the members will become bored, and the truth of the lesson will be lost. It will be interesting if it is in the range of their knowledge and touches areas in which they need help. (It may be well, at this point, to reread the list of adjustments young people are making which is presented in chap. 3.)

Young people are concerned about things pertaining to education, a vocation, economic independence, dating, parenthood, service in the armed forces, and many other areas.

Something in one of these vital areas may be related to the lesson for the day. Knowing the natural interest of his class members in such an area will guide the teacher in tying that in with the central truth of the lesson.

He may do this by showing the class a book, a picture, or an object. He may write a word on the board. It may suit his need better to read a letter from a missionary, a newspaper headline, a clipping from the want ad section of the newspaper, or to refer to a line from his favorite cartoon character. Perhaps he may get attention best by using a poster made by a member of the class which will remain before the group as the lesson is taught. He may ask a question which will provoke thought and discussion.

The writer was asked to teach an Adult men's Sunday school class at Ridgecrest Assembly one summer. The lesson was a biographical study of Ruth. Not until preparing the lesson did it occur to the teacher that the three men mentioned first in the book have died by the time one has finished reading the first five verses.

The lesson could not begin with the funerals of three men and attract much interest from a class of males.

But by reading the opening chapter many times it became obvious that the series of events leading to the marriage of Ruth and Boaz began when Elimelech and Naomi, with their sons Mahlon and Chilion, moved to Moab.

It was logical then to begin the lesson with the question, "When should a family move?" The answers were so immediate and interesting it was difficult to direct attention to the actual study of the lesson itself.

The members will not learn if they are inattentive and disinterested. The teacher must put forth his best efforts from the very start of the lesson period.

2. *Guide Attention into Sustained Interest*

Attention may be likened to the pendulum of a clock. It swings back and forth from what the teacher is saying and doing to other things. What the teacher says may remind a pupil of something in which he has a greater interest. He may pursue this idea for a time until he becomes conscious of his activity, and then his attention reverts to what the teacher is saying.

So much may have transpired in the interlude that he begins to wonder how the teacher has prepared such a disconnected lesson. The lesson may be perfectly logical. It is he who has gone astray.

The best students find difficulty in concentrating their attention upon one thought or idea very long. Thus one of the great problems of teaching is to guide attention into the realm of sustained interest when the mind is holding the main ideas in the center of consciousness over a period of time.

3. *Procedure Subject to Change*

In beginning a lesson the teacher may find that his introduction is failing to get the attention he had planned. He will have to decide whether he shall use the planned introduction or shift to something else. Often a statement or an experience related by one of the members at the beginning of the class period gives him something better than he had planned to use. But no teacher should go to his class trusting that something of such nature will play into his hands. Success will come by planning constructively in advance.

As the teacher begins the lesson he should remember that young people are alert and curious. They are interested in whatever has action or offers them an active part. They revel in what is new and varied. Interest is contagious. If some are more interested than others, the teacher should capitalize upon their interest. An expression of interest will be beneficial to those who are less interested.

IV. Getting Participation

It has been estimated that individuals retain 5 per cent of what they hear, 40 per cent of what they see, but 90 per cent of what they do. All three of these media should be used in teaching, especially the latter.

When the lesson is properly introduced, the teacher then is ready to continue the learning process. This he will do, trying as much as possible to get the class members to engage in activities which will contribute to their learning.

1. *Call for Assignments*

As the lesson is taught, the teacher should make use of any assignments which he has made previously. This should be done in such a way as to cause the other class members to feel they are not listening to reports. If the ones who had the assignments can be used in the class discussion informally, their contributions will not appear mechanical. This will encourage the others to participate.

2. *Use the Bible*

The teacher must seek to get the class members to use their Bibles. If the entire lesson passage is read, the teacher will encourage each member to open his Bible and follow the reading. He will find many uses for the Bible as the lesson study proceeds. He may ask the members to read certain Scripture references in proof of the truth of the passage being studied. He may use it to raise questions and answer them. The Bible may be read for an authoritative statement, "Thus saith the Lord." If the members read the Scripture passage themselves, this activity will help them to understand its truth.

3. Encourage Questions

Participation is secured also by letting the members know their questions are welcomed. Some teachers fear questions and object to their pupils raising them. Some believe questions will "get them off the lesson." In reality a sincere question is the lesson for the one who asks it. If the teacher is bound rigidly by an outline, it is a rather clear indication that he teaches lessons rather than the class members.

Of course, all questions will not be important enough to take the time of the class to answer. But the teacher should show his interest in all of them. He may answer those of value to the group in class and indicate his willingness to discuss the other questions with individual members at a time convenient to them.

4. Direct Discussion

If a discussion is planned, or if one arises during the lesson period, the teacher should give guidance to it, but should not be dictatorial in his attitude. When he asks for discussions, he may get quite a bit which is not directly related to the topic being discussed. Also he may get adverse opinions.

To all of these he must keep a tolerant attitude. This does not mean he must agree with all which is said. Quite the opposite is true. He will not declare himself early in the discussion, but draw all the information possible from the class members, letting them form their own opinions as the topic is discussed.

The discussion must be kept moving. This may be done by not permitting one or more members to dominate the discussion. The teacher may have to intervene if a member consumes more than his share of the time.

Exchange of opinion should include all members of the

class. The teacher should watch for any indication of interest on the part of individuals who are not participating. He should seek to get these members to join him in the discussion. If some are timid and hesitant, he should endeavor to get them to take part. But he should not embarrass them by calling upon them if they are not ready to participate.

Discussion will be facilitated if the teacher works, at first, with a small group in the class. The class officers and other interested members will form a fine nucleus with which to work. If these are encouraged to do their share of learning activities, other members of the class will follow their example.

5. *Watch the Time*

The teacher has only thirty or forty minutes in which to teach the lesson. He must always be conscious of the time element without making it too obvious to the class members. If he is constantly saying, "We don't have time" or "We have to hurry on," he will destroy the pleasure of Bible study.

If he is lecturing, he may control the use of the time better than if he uses other methods. But he must train himself to decide quickly what is important and what unimportant, so that he will know how to achieve the most with the time he has.

As a rule the teacher of young people will not be confronted with the problem of a talkative class member. If he should face this problem he must learn how to interrupt such a person tactfully after he has talked beyond the point of contributing to the discussion. Class members may be used by the teacher to keep one person from dominating the study period of the class. He may encourage all members to take part by asking them for their opinions.

V. Arriving at Worth-while Conclusions

Arriving at one's destination is the most important phase of making a journey. It is no less important in teaching. The teacher at all times must be seeking to lead his class to attain something worth while for themselves.

1. Remembering the Aim

As the teacher teaches, he is keeping before him his aim or goal. He has a mission to perform, a purpose to accomplish. He does not drive on toward it unconscious of the reactions of his class. If they are moving with him, well and good. But progress may not be without interruption or delay. The teacher must keep in contact with his class.

If the aim is accurate, and the teaching satisfactory, certain worth-while conclusions will be reached by the members of the class. If these conclusions are vivid and real, they will find their way into conduct. This is the real purpose of teaching.

As a young man, the writer went forward at the close of the Sunday morning service and told his pastor he enjoyed his sermon. Gripping his hand firmly, the pastor asked, "What are you going to do about it?" It was the first time it had ever occurred to this young man that he was supposed to do something about a sermon. There was no answer immediately forthcoming, but a lesson was taught which was never forgotten. Every preacher and teacher is anxious for his ministry to produce results in the lives of others. He wants something done about his preaching or teaching.

2. Testing Conclusions with Bible Truth

In trying to arrive at helpful conclusions the teacher has a variety of choices. He may sum up the discussion or lead the members of the class to do so. This may lead to further discussion which will resolve differences of opinion that have developed. It is not necessary to secure the agreement of all the members on certain conclusions. Some may disagree with the majority. If this is done in a good spirit, it may stimulate further learning on the part of all.

However, all conclusions reached must be evaluated in terms of Bible truth. There is always the problem of accepting conclusions which may fall short of the Bible standard of belief or conduct.

It is often a good plan to ask each member to express himself regarding the contribution which the lesson has made to him. The teacher or a class member may write these on the board as they are indicated.

When the central truth of a lesson is understood, it may be well for the teacher to raise a question, such as "Now, what would it cost us to apply this?" or "What would applying this truth demand of us?"

3. *An Example from the Teaching of Jesus*

Motivating the members to act upon the truth they have learned is a part of all good teaching. When Christ concluded the "Lesson" on the Mount, he did so with an appeal to action: "Therefore whosoever heareth these sayings of mine, and doeth them, I will liken him unto a wise man, which built his house upon a rock: . . . and everyone that heareth these sayings of mine, and doeth them not, shall be likened unto a foolish man, which built his house upon the sand" (Matt. 7:24, 26).

The first man chose the right foundation by accepting the teaching of Christ. The second man chose the wrong foundation for his life by rejecting the teaching of Christ. The differences made by the choices of these two men were apparent to Jesus' hearers.

All the people were familiar with the importance of

the right foundation for a house. They knew the difference in rock and sand for a foundation. They knew the destructive power of floods and winds. Jesus used their knowledge of things about them to lead them to the new knowledge of building one's life on the right foundation so that it might stand under the storm and stress which comes to each individual.

VI. STIMULATING FURTHER LEARNING

The teacher is not called upon to settle everything in the classroom. Rather, it is his responsibility to make the lesson period so stimulating the members will think of the lesson truth again and again during the week. Each lesson should leave the members hungry for more truth.

1. *"Closing" Each Lesson Unnecessary*

Learning may be aided if the teacher will not attempt to "close" each lesson. Many questions will need further study before they may be answered correctly. Someone should be given the responsibility of looking up the answers. He must be guided to the proper source of information.

If the class is having a business meeting during the week, perhaps the discussion may be continued there with suggestions made by the teacher as to further reading and study of the subject.

Where a question of doctrine is involved, the pastor, a deacon, or some other well-prepared member of the church would be glad to suggest sources of information to the teacher. In certain instances special meetings might be arranged with one of these leaders guiding the discussion. Materials in tract, pamphlet, or book form may be suggested for further study. The church librarian is helpful in this area.

2. *Capitalizing upon Pupil Interest*

Books and articles in denominational papers, when they relate to the lessons being studied, may be used to challenge young people who are willing to do some research.

When the teacher knows the school life of his class members, their vocational problems and achievements, and their relationships as parents or with their own parents, he can establish certain relationships with these areas of life and the lesson series, and so secure a carry-over of learnings into weekday living.

If the teacher will discover what there is of major interest to his members in the lesson for next Sunday, he can whet their appetites for study. If he will keep the lessons related to one another and to the unit, the teacher can make each member feel a need to study any lesson which he may have missed. The importance of Bible study is minimized if young people are expected to study only when they attend.

FOR FURTHER STUDY

1. Consider your classroom and its equipment. What can you do to improve the environment of teaching—rearrange the equipment, get additional equipment, make the room more attractive?
2. Think of the past four lessons you have taught. How did you introduce them? Have the introductions been too similar? Plan for a new approach next Sunday.
3. Are your members responsive or unresponsive in class? What can you do to get them to participate in the lesson next Sunday?
4. Does your teaching cause the pupils to arrive at worthwhile conclusions? How have several lesson periods ended recently? Is there room for improvement here?

CHAPTER 8

I. REASONS FOR EVALUATING TEACHING

   1. To Measure the Growth of Class Members
   2. To Find Out What Class Members Need
   3. To Locate Difficulties in the Learning Process
   4. To Lift the Level of Teaching

II. EVIDENCES OF SUCCESSFUL TEACHING

   1. Numerical Growth
   2. Attendance
   3. Bible Knowledge
   4. Attention and Interest in the Class
   5. The Individual Grade
   6. The Class Standard of Excellence
   7. Evangelism and Church Membership
   8. Personal Growth of Class Members

III. THE TEACHER HAS HELPERS IN EVALUATING HIS TEACHING

   1. The Pastor and Other Staff Members
   2. The Superintendents and Young People Themselves

IV. TEACHING SUCCEEDS AS THE TEACHER GROWS

   1. Some Questions to Answer
   2. Paul's Exhortation

8

Evidences of Successful Teaching

And Jesus increased in wisdom and stature, and in favour with God and man (Luke 2:52)

It is DIFFICULT for a teacher to know when he has taught. The department superintendent may know he has served as an administrator when he conducts meetings, organizes new classes, and enlists new workers. A secretary may know he has served when the records are carefully totaled and the proper reports are made. But proving that one has taught involves more than simply meeting a class each Sunday. At the close of each lesson period it is difficult for the teacher to know whether or not he has taught. Yet he must be anxious to know the results of his teaching. He, more than anyone else, should try to determine how successful his efforts are. His teaching is being tested whether he realizes it or not.

Two friends were discussing the salaries of football coaches in relation to the salaries of professors in colleges and universities. One objected to the disproportionate salaries paid to the football coaches. After some thought the other observed that if the teaching of the professors was being tested every Saturday afternoon by as many thousands of people as the teaching of the coaches, the best of them might receive better salaries. The truth is, their work is being tested. But, unlike the football coaches, their immediate tenure of office is not determined by the efficiency of their teaching.

A new degree of teaching efficiency will come in the Sunday school when teachers realize their teaching is tested.

I. Reasons for Evaluating Teaching

Several reasons for evaluating teaching are apparent as one considers the subject.

1. *To Measure the Growth of Class Members*

The Sunday school teacher is concerned with the growth of the total personality of his class members. He is anxious for each one to be well adjusted to the members of his family and the ones with whom he associates in school or in business. He wants each member to have a sense of inner security and peace. He desires that each one form habits of health which will lead him to have a strong body with which to work and serve. He wants each member to overcome any personal handicaps which would hinder him in reaching his greatest usefulness.

But the teacher should be concerned most with the spiritual growth of each member. Is he a Christian? Is he growing in Christlikeness? Stated in different terms, has he accepted Christ as his personal Saviour? Has he taken Christ as his example in life? Is he striving to be a better church member each day? Each teacher should look especially for evidences that his members are increasing "in favour with God." It is possible for a teacher to teach each Sunday and not be aware that this is the most important information for him to possess. He must get some accurate idea of growth in this field if he succeeds.

2. *To Find Out What Class Members Need*

If a teacher knows the life needs of his members, he may focus his teaching upon meeting these needs. Guesswork in this area should be avoided. Time spent in evaluating his work will cause each teacher to concentrate his efforts where they will accomplish the greatest success.

It is recommended that each person have a physical checkup at least once a year. If he does so, the physician checks him carefully to discover if his body is functioning properly. If something is discovered which must be corrected, the physician then prescribes the remedy.

A teacher, like a medical doctor, should become as expert as possible in diagnosis. Often he will discover certain needs of his pupils which must be corrected. Some needs may be so serious as to demand the additional help of the pastor and perhaps others in the community. Other needs may be such as to be corrected through good teaching and additional encouragement and help outside the classroom.

But every teacher should strive to know what the important needs of the members are. It is only through this knowledge that he will be able to determine the direction and emphasis of his teaching.

3. *To Locate Difficulties in the Learning Process*

There are many difficulties in the way of successful teaching. Some of these lie within the members themselves. It is possible they have grown up without any real interest in Bible study. Some may not have learned how to study in the public school; therefore no real study habits have been formed. Some may have little ambition. In the same class the teacher may have some brilliant pupils, some with average intelligence, and others who are below normal in ability to learn.

The environment of teaching may be a great hindrance to the learning process. The room may be too small and improperly ventilated. The chairs may be uncomfortable. The pupils may have to face direct light. All classes may have to meet in the church auditorium, where there is much noise and confusion. In some churches where there are individual rooms, the partitions between them may be so thin that there will be much interference from the classes in adjoining rooms.

It is important to understand the difficulties and seek to remedy them.

As the teacher evaluates his work, he may find some of the difficulties are chargeable to him. He may not know the pupils well. He may not have formed good study habits himself. He may not be skilled in the use of teaching methods and materials.

Most teachers will discover problems in all these areas. Their discovery and a frank facing of them are important steps in improving the learning process.

4. *To Lift the Level of Teaching*

The largest room in any church is the room for improvement. As long as teachers are satisfied with the number of members they have and the quality of work they are doing, the class will not grow and the level of work will not be lifted. When the workers are filled with "a holy discontent," the quality of work will begin to improve.

"The old-time religion" is good enough for everybody, but it must be presented in the finest, most attractive, and up-to-date ways which can be discovered. This fact should keep every teacher at work seeking to find a better way of presenting the timeless truth. When one knows what the weaknesses in his teaching are, he may begin planning and projecting a program of improvement. It is only in this way that his teaching will result in success.

II. EVIDENCES OF SUCCESSFUL TEACHING

While it is manifestly impossible to determine always what degree of success a teacher achieves, there are some practical signs of success that may be observed.

1. *Numerical Growth*

One test of successful teaching is the increase in class enrolment. This applies of course to the class which has prospects for its membership. A teacher is succeeding if the members of the class become concerned enough to join with him in visiting their prospective members.

It is never easy to enlist young people. So a teacher should not be discouraged if the prospects are slow to respond. If the members are working systematically, the act of enrolling will take care of itself. But over a period of several months the class should have visitors and new members. If this is not taking place, the teacher and class members should ask and answer the question, "Why?"

Mrs. H. E. Barnett, who for thirty-two years has taught seventeen-year-old young women in the Sunday school of the First Baptist Church, San Antonio, Texas, has never failed in any year to double the enrolment of her class by the end of the first quarter, and to triple it by the end of the year. She has said she would know her work was finished if she failed in any year to accomplish these goals.

This is a remarkable record and not every teacher, even with diligent effort, would succeed as she has done. But this experience indicates what may be accomplished when a teacher takes enlistment as an evidence of successful teaching.

2. *Attendance*

For a long time, attendance has been a recognized means of measuring successful teaching. Increase in attendance and the maintenance of a good average attendance are indicative of interest. But, by themselves, they are not conclusive evidence of success in teaching. Attendance may be stimulated artificially by offering rewards and sponsoring contests. Ties of fellowship are strong, and young people may be attending because of this appeal. Social activities, athletic teams, and other things, while important and necessary even from the standpoint of learning opportunities, may be more responsible for attendance than the more important Bible study opportunities in the class.

When the class is functioning as it should, and the teacher is majoring upon interesting Bible study, attendance is a fairly accurate test. Normally, when a person is regular in attendance, he is interested in what his class is doing.

Near a college campus, where there is frequently an exodus to near-by homes on week ends, the attendance will run lower as a rule than in more normal situations. Every effort should be made to encourage the students to be faithful in their attendance. Each teacher should check the average attendance of his class for the past year and determine what the records reveal.

3. Bible Knowledge

The young person's growth in Bible knowledge is an excellent test of teaching. This is one of the principal goals of the teacher. Attaining Bible knowledge is an important aim of teaching. But incorporating this knowledge into daily living is also of vital concern to teacher and pupil. Knowing and applying the truth go hand in hand. The member must know the truth before he can act upon it. Paul wrote, "So then faith cometh by hearing, and hearing by the word of God" (Rom. 10:17).

It is somewhat difficult to know with accuracy the extent of one's knowledge of the Bible. Certain Bible knowledge tests have been developed but have been very limited in use.

It is possible for teachers to work out objective tests

with true-false, completion, best-answer questions, and also the matching of statements. Such a test could be used for testing the teaching of a quarter's lessons. It could be given on the last Sunday of the quarter preceded by a review of the entire study. Something of this nature would require more study, and test the Bible knowledge retained by the class members following their study. Preparing such tests accurately requires a knowledge of test construction which many Sunday school teachers do not possess. There are excellent books on the subject and public and college teachers can give advice and counsel regarding the construction of objective tests.

The teachers may learn the extent of Bible knowledge by preparing questions which may be asked and answered orally in class. This may be done somewhat frequently in the regular sessions of the class. More questions than usual could be used on the last Sunday of the quarter to determine the information of the pupils regarding the entire unit. This method would have to be varied of course.

The teacher might lead the members to prepare short papers based upon the quarter's lessons. This would require a review study of all the lessons. Such a study would unify the individual's knowledge of the series and give him a more comprehensive understanding of it. This procedure would help the teacher to determine if the study of the lessons had been meaningful to the members.

4. *Attention and Interest in the Class*

The attention and interest shown by members in the classroom is a test of effective teaching. No one can teach when there is inattention. Young people are so interested in one another that they may engage in conversation among themselves while the teacher is trying to teach.

Although this is one of the worst forms of rudeness, a teacher cannot afford to be rude in the way he seeks to get their attention. He must work for it in the classroom and do what he can to improve the situation through his contacts with class members outside the class period.

Regardless of how long it may take the teacher to accomplish it, the attention of his members must be his goal. Learning cannot take place without attention.

If the young people ask questions, contribute to the information of their fellow members, and take part in the various activities of the lesson period, the teacher may know his teaching is meeting the test of interest.

5. *The Individual Grade*

The grade of the member on the Six Point Record System has been used as a sole test of successful teaching by some teachers. An overemphasis on a 100 per cent class has led many classes to adopt the policy of removing names from the roll when members do not attend three successive Sundays. This practice reveals a complete misunderstanding of the purpose of the Six Point Record System. It is designed to encourage every member to cultivate six important habits. If a member has formed none of these habits, the teacher and class have work to do. Christ said, "They that are whole have no need of the physician, but they that are sick" (Mark 2:17).

Some teachers have been known to discourage certain individuals from joining their classes for fear they would not help to maintain a high class grade. Getting a disinterested member to become active and worthy is a teacher's great opportunity. If a choice has to be made, it is far better for the class grade to be low and the teacher's record of responsibility to be pleasing to God.

The grade a person makes each Sunday is certainly one test of teaching. However, if the member fails to make a good record on certain points, his failure will indicate his need for the teacher's assistance. Of course he cannot be taught if he is absent. If he is late on Sunday, he will miss the preparation for teaching him through the assembly period. He should bring his own Bible to class after having studied it during the week. He needs to make an offering regularly. If he does not stay for the morning worship service, he misses the climactic service of the morning with all the opportunities of worship, learning, and commitment which it affords. Weakness on all or any of these points represents work for the teacher. As the grade of the member improves, the teacher may take this as an evidence of success with that person.

Every teacher should have an enthusiastic attitude toward the record system and should use his influence in making its use more effective in his class.

6. *The Class Standard of Excellence*

Reaching and maintaining the Standard of Excellence for Young People's classes, if not a test of successful teaching, is a test of the teacher's leadership. It will require time and effort by the teacher to lead the class to reach this objective. Even if it is not attained, its adoption as a program of work and a measurement of the progress being made will create better opportunities for learning.

Following the Standard will keep the class from going off on tangents and will offer a balanced set of procedures which have been tested and proved through use by hundreds of churches.

The frequent use of the Standard of Excellence as a measuring device will indicate both the accomplishments and the work which remains to be done. Once it has been reached, frequent checking should be done to make sure it is being maintained.

7. *Evangelism and Church Membership*

Evidence of successful teaching may be found in the number of unsaved members enrolled. But even so, the teacher should be positively evangelistic and should be seeking to win each of his unsaved members to Christ.

If all class members are Christians, the teacher should lead them to locate unsaved prospects and win them to Christ. Most classes have many unsaved possibilities. Winning them should be the major objective of every class.

In addition to unsaved members and prospects, the class may have several unaffiliated Baptist class members and prospects. Definite effort should be put forth to enlist them in church membership.

If a class is constantly reaching out toward the unsaved and unaffiliated in its community, it is indicative of a teacher whose teaching is being directed toward the central objective.

8. *Personal Growth of Class Members*

Successful teaching is evidenced by the changed lives of the class members.

(1) *The growth of religious ideals.*—Whatever else the teacher does, he should give his class members the highest possible ideals. Each young person should develop ideals of giving, serving, sacrificing, sharing, and living for Christ. The teacher will not accomplish this by formal teaching alone but by the power of his own life and example.

The growth of ideals depends upon the desire which is created for them. The teacher must make Christian living appealing and attractive. It should be so desirable members of the class will be willing to pay a price to achieve it.

Because ideals are subjective, it is difficult to know if

they are being cultivated in the lives of one's members. However, in a class where the teacher is maintaining a personal contact with those enrolled, it is possible to note progress along this line. As members express their ambitions and goals, the teacher will have some idea of his success.

(2) *The development of right attitudes.*—Life is controlled largely by attitudes. A person's attitude toward himself is important. If he overestimates or underestimates himself, he will face difficulties in making adjustments to life.

One's attitudes toward others is important also. If a person has little regard for the life and property of another, he becomes a criminal or a thief. If he has a high regard for personality and property, he will become a useful citizen. Paul wrote, "For I say, through the grace given unto me, to every man that is among you, not to think of himself more highly than he ought to think; but to think soberly, according as God hath dealt to every man the measure of faith" (Rom. 12: 3).

Attitudes will be expressed in private conversation and in class. They will be revealed in the actions of the members also. If one of the members has been inclined toward egotism, the teacher will be watching for some sign of humility. If two members dislike each other, the teacher will be hopeful of signs of friendliness. If some have had the wrong attitudes toward those of other races, the teacher will be anxious to note the growth of a Christian attitude. These illustrations could be multiplied, but they indicate what evaluation in this area can mean.

(3) *The achievement of Christian character.*—A person's character is what he is under all circumstances and conditions. It is the sum of all his capacities, attitudes, habits, and choices. Effective teaching assists individuals in mastering bad habits. It guides them in developing good habits in their stead.

It is important for each teacher to discover weaknesses in the character of each member and lead him to overcome them. As young people become stable in character, a teacher may know he is succeeding in his task.

Teachers and members are dependent upon the Holy Spirit as they work for the transformation of life and character. They must look to him for leadership and power for the task. The promise of the presence of the Holy Spirit is as definite today as it was to the early Christians, "Ye shall receive power, after that the Holy Ghost is come upon you: and ye shall be witnesses unto me" (Acts 1:8).

(4) *The expression of right conduct.*—What a person is will be revealed by what he does. Each member should be directed toward living a life of Christian stewardship. His life should be like Paul's who was able to say, "For to me to live is Christ" (Phil. 1:21). Each Christian must be careful to guard his Christian influence. Certain things might not be harmful to him, but they would cause those who are weaker than he is to go astray.

Paul set the example when he wrote, "Wherefore, if meat make my brother to offend, I will eat no flesh while the world standeth, lest I make my brother to offend" (1 Cor. 8:13). Each Christian must evaluate his influence so that he may use it in keeping others pointed toward Christ.

What the pupil does with his material possessions is another test of successful teaching. If he realizes he is a steward and is growing in the grace of giving, the teacher may feel he is learning the Christian way of life. Young people often are guilty of spending more money on amusements each week than they give to the work of the kingdom. Teaching of the right type will lead them away from such practice.

In due time all young people should be led to give a tenth of their incomes as a minimum. Even when they reach this goal (and ultimately, many should go beyond this with their offerings) they should realize they are stewards of the nine-tenths also.

Are members selfish and covetous? Are they living primarily for pleasure? Are they spending their money with little regard for spiritual values? If so, much teaching remains to be done.

What young people are doing with their talents is another test of teaching. Is the one-talent member using that one for the glory of God? Is the five-talent member investing his talents wisely? Is the ten-talent member using all ten in the service of Christ? Each teacher should know the talents of his members and should determine to what extent they are being wasted, developed, or completely yielded in consecrated service.

The use of time greatly affects one's conduct. Do members of the class waste time, or have they learned it is essence of life itself? Do they spend it idly, or are they using it constructively? Do they take time to study their Bibles, pray, and seek to discover God's will for their lives? By seeking for answers to these questions the teacher will be evaluating his teaching.

III. The Teacher Has Helpers in Evaluating His Teaching

The discussion thus far has indicated the ways in which the teacher may evaluate his work. It should be remembered there are several leaders in the church who will be happy to assist him in measuring and improving his ministry.

1. *The Pastor and Other Staff Members*

The pastor, with his training, experience, and understanding, is a constant and sympathetic friend of every teacher. His knowledge of the Bible, of young people, and of teaching procedures makes him a valued counselor and guide. He is busy, so his time must be protected and respected; but he is always eager and ready to help.

The minister of education and other full-time vocational workers in the larger churches are trained and skilled in this work. Fortunate is the church which has one or more such persons on its staff. A teacher who desires and seeks the help and direction of such a worker will find guidance in the best ways to improve his work. Accepting the suggestions of these staff members will assist them in accomplishing their ministry in the church.

2. *The Superintendents and Young People Themselves*

The general and department superintendents of the Sunday school are fellow workers in the improvement of the quality of work in the Sunday school. Their task is to aid every teacher in achieving his maximum contributions for Christ.

If the teacher feels free to do so, he may ask for constructive criticism from the young people themselves. They are very frank as a rule, and if the teacher will put his feelings in the background, his class members will render him a real service. To see himself as they see him will go a long way toward making him a better worker.

When a teacher approaches the leadership of the church or the membership of his class for counsel, he should accept suggestions as they are given him. If he freely admits his need, and even the best workers need to improve, he will be happy in this comradeship of learning.

IV. Teaching Succeeds as the Teacher Grows

The teacher is the most important factor in the teaching process. Successful teaching depends upon him.

The teacher should answer objectively such questions as the following: Is there a real spirit of fellowship existing between me and each member of my class? Do I maintain a personal contact with each one through visitation? Am I mastering the techniques of lesson preparation? Do I have the members in mind when I study? Am I ambitious for the spiritual growth of each young person? Is my life the proper example for them? Am I seeking to win unsaved and unaffiliated members to Christ and church membership? Am I growing in teaching ability? Am I satisfied with the results of my teaching? Am I a growing Christian?

Each teacher should be able to answer the majority of these questions affirmatively. If he cannot do so he should put forth extra effort to develop his own life and improve the quality of his work.

FOR FURTHER STUDY

1. Ask the secretary of your class to give you the average attendance of the class for the past three months. Compare this with the enrolment. What do these facts reveal?
2. Can you say definitely that your members are growing in knowledge of the Bible? Upon what do you base your answer?
3. How many unsaved and unaffiliated members are enrolled in your class? How many unsaved and unaffiliated prospects do you have? What plans do you have for winning them to Christ and church membership?
4. Do you have evidences of the personal growth of your class members—in use of time, in giving of money, in dedication of talents, and in desire to serve?

CHAPTER 9

9

The Teacher's Interpersonal Relationships

But I am among you as he that serveth
(Luke 22:27)

THE SIGNIFICANCE of interpersonal relationships is assuming more and more importance in society. If an individual cannot "get along" with his fellows, he will not develop and mature properly. Unless he is accepted by others, it will be impossible for him to achieve the fullest happiness and success. The business institutions of the nation are giving attention to adjusting people in their work and helping them in their associations with their fellow workers.

Teaching is a relationship of persons. The success of the teacher will depend upon being accepted and appreciated by others. This applies not only to his being accepted by the members of the class but by others in the church and community as well. The teacher who does not care what others think of him does not realize how dependent he is upon others for his personal growth and usefulness.

The success of the teacher depends not only upon his ability to relate himself to others, but upon his success in relating others to a personal Saviour. His usefulness hinges on the extent of his love for God and his fellow man and his willingness to serve them.

Since the work of the teacher is concerned with persons and a personal God, each teacher needs a pattern for establishing and maintaining the right interpersonal relationships.

I. PATTERNED AFTER THE EXAMPLE OF CHRIST

The teacher who succeeds must take Christ as his example, not only in teaching but in the other areas of life as well. Christ had to deal with individuals who were ignorant and prejudiced. He had to meet problems growing out of social distinctions, religious bigotry, and racial hatred.

But Christ never alienated anyone deliberately. Those who became his enemies did so through their own choice. The friends he made were not his friends through superficial promises or overtures. He had given them salvation, a new life, new happiness, and new hope.

When one is serving Christ, he must master his desire for personal gain or recognition. Even the disciples disputed among themselves as to who should be the greatest in the kingdom. Christ used this incident to teach them that first place in his kingdom came as the result of service (Luke 22:24–27).

Christ dramatized humility by taking a basin and a towel and washing his disciples' feet (John 13:3–16). This was a task performed by servants. No servant was present at this feast, and the disciples had not been thoughtful enough to wash each other's feet, or they were too proud to do so. But Jesus looked upon this situation as an opportunity to serve.

The effect of this act of humility is as strong today as it was at the moment of its performance. This is shown by the following quotation from the preaching of A. E. Whitham as given by Alexander Gammie:

On my return (from a visit to a museum) I must have dozed, for I thought I was treading the streets of the Holy City, pottering about like a tourist. In my wanderings I came upon the museum of that city of our dreams. I went in, and a courteous attendant conducted me round. There was some old armour there, much bruised with battle. Many things were conspicuous by their absence. I saw nothing of Alexander's nor of Napoleon's. There was no Pope's ring, nor even the ink-bottle that Luther is said to have thrown at the devil, nor Wesley's seal and keys, nor the first minutes of the Conference, nor the last (I was sorry about that, because my name was in it). I saw a widow's mite and the feather of a little bird. I saw some swaddling-clothes, a hammer and three nails, and a few thorns. I saw a bit of fishing net and the broken oar of a boat. I saw a sponge that had once been dipped in vinegar, and a small piece of silver. But I cannot enumerate or describe all I felt. Whilst I was turning over a common drinking cup which had a very honourable place, I whispered to the attendant, "Have you got a towel and a basin among your collection?" "No," he answered, "not here; you see they are in constant use." Then I knew I was in Heaven, the Holy City and amid the redeemed society. Knowing that He came from God and went to God . . . [He] took a towel and a basin.[1]

Jesus made clear to his disciples that following him involved self-denial and sacrifice. He said to them, "If any man will come after me, let him deny himself, and take up his cross, and follow me. For whosoever will save his life shall lose it: and whosoever will lose his life for my sake shall find it" (Matt. 16:24–25).

Serving Christ is not for personal advancement but to advance his work through giving oneself to others.

II. In Harmony with the Leadership of the Church

The pastor, other vocational workers in the church such as the minister of religious education and educational secretary, the deacons, the general superintendent, and the department superintendent are leaders of the church with whom the young people's teacher will serve.

---

[1] Alexander Gammie, *Preachers I Have Heard* (London: Pickering and Inglis, Ltd., 1945), pp. 120–121. Used by permission.

These are entitled to the full support of each worker. For any teacher to be critical, sensitive, or stubborn creates unnecessary problems for these leaders.

The interests of the church, the Sunday school, and the department must be considered as greater than the particular interests of any teacher or class. Certainly a teacher should not use his position or influence to secure some concession for his class which would hinder the progress of other classes in the Sunday school. What is best for the church, the Sunday school, and the department should receive the support of the teacher. The teacher should co-operate in such matters as changing the name of his class, moving to a new classroom, or completely reorganizing the department or class if the leadership of the church feels these things should be done.

Every worker should feel free to express himself when these and other matters are being discussed. If the teacher is opposed to any plan, he should register his opposition. He should do so in a spirit of Christian kindliness without being personal or seeking deliberately to hurt the feelings of anyone. But if he is in the minority when the vote is taken, he should demonstrate the right spirit by staying in harmony with his fellow workers.

No teacher should impose upon the time of his leaders by idle talk or vain repetition. He should not demand any special attention or recognition. Rather, he should be considerate of those in positions of leadership, seeking to understand them and interpret them properly to the young people in his class.

III. IN FELLOWSHIP WITH THE MEMBERS OF THE CHURCH

A spirit of fellowship and agreement is essential in building a strong church. The teacher of young people must contribute to such a spirit. If there is ill will or animosity between individuals in the church, it will have its effect on the entire membership. The children of Israel suffered because of Achan's sin. The wrong spirit in a church will keep it from accomplishing its mission in the community.

God has given great victories when his people have been united. Gideon won his victory with 300 men because "they stood every man in his place round about the camp" (Judg. 7:21). Nehemiah rebuilt the wall, "for the people had a mind to work" (Neh. 4:6). On the day of Pentecost the early Christians "were all with one accord in one place" (Acts 2:1).

The things which keep church members fighting among themselves are trivial as a rule. If members had been big enough, they would have overlooked them. If all the energies of Christian people could be spent in fighting the devil instead of fighting one another, greater gains would be made in doing the work of Christ.

Not long ago the chairman of a church building and grounds committee related an interesting experience. In trying to find a suitable location for a new Nursery department, the committee of which he was chairman located a room without outside ventilation. At the time they discovered it, it was being used for storage. The chairman, in telling of the incident, stated that he was violently opposed to the use of this room as a Nursery. The other members were just as convinced it should be used for this purpose.

During their meeting the chairman became so emotionally disturbed, he abruptly left the others and went home rather than display his emotions more violently. That night as he sat in his living room, he realized he had made a mistake. If the others were unanimous in feeling the room should be used, he should not bring in a minority report to the church.

He owned a successful furniture store in his city. He began to think of ways in which the room might be made attractive and inviting as a Nursery.

Calling the members of the committee together again (and they must have come reluctantly), he apologized to them for his conduct and said, "If you are still convinced the room should be used as a Nursery, I will put covering on the floor at no expense to the church and will do everything I can to make the room usable."

This demonstration saved a difficult situation in the church and led to greater progress for the Sunday school.

The attitude of a teacher will soon become the attitude of the class. To alienate young people from other church members and the church is a serious matter. To attract them to the church and its members is very important. When one loves his church, is in fellowship with its members, and gives it his full support, he is teaching by the depth of his loyalties and convictions.

IV. LEARNING THROUGH CONTACTS WITH HIS FELLOW WORKERS

It would be interesting to know how much one learns from his contacts with others. Much knowledge and understanding come in this manner. Frequent contacts of workers for sharing knowledge and experience will be enriching.

Perhaps the best opportunity for this comes through the weekly officers and teachers' meeting. Each Sunday school should establish and maintain such a meeting for the contributions it may make to the growth and development of the workers. Through praying, planning, and studying together, the officers and teachers will find that many profitable experiences are made possible.

If such a meeting is provided each week, certainly each

teacher should show his appreciation and interest by attending the meeting and taking part in the various phases of the program. Preparation before one attends will cause him to get greater benefits from the meeting.

Sometimes experienced workers do not attend because they feel the meeting does not offer them enough help. The superintendent is responsible for planning something worthwhile for every meeting. But one should not attend simply to get something, although he is entitled to receive something every time he comes. If he attends to share his information and experience with his fellow workers, and listens as they share what they know with him, he will find the meeting has been of value.

Taking part in training course activities is another means of learning through group experiences. An increasing number of churches are making adequate provision for the training of their workers.

There is value in meeting together periodically for such study. Each book in the Church Study Course represents the accumulated knowledge and experience of its author. It contains helpful guidance suggestions for the teacher of the study course. Usually the book is taught by a person who has more than average ability and information. The discussion of the members in which ideas and experiences are shared will mean additional learning opportunities.

There is comradeship in learning. When a group of teachers join in a quest for greater knowledge of the Bible, Baptist doctrine, teaching methods, Sunday school administration, and other subjects, contributions will be made to the lives of all.

Each teacher should keep in touch with the superintendent of training so that he will know at all times the books to be studied for the completion of diplomas and seals. He should join with others in requesting that books be taught at a time when the majority of the workers may study them. He should study training course books at home if classes cannot be conducted as often as he feels the need for study.

When books are offered, he should arrange his daily activities so he may take advantage of joining with others in the study. Every worthy task requires a trained personnel. Sunday school teaching is an art requiring all the knowledge and experience one may bring to the classroom. Learning through a joint activity is an excellent means of qualifying for this task.

V. PLACING THE INTERESTS OF HIS MEMBERS ABOVE HIS OWN

Christ "came not to be ministered unto, but to minister" (Matt. 20:28). Serving others should be the principal desire of every teacher. Working with youth just to "stay young" or to be identified with youthful activities are not, in themselves, sufficient reasons for teaching such a group. If one succeeds as a teacher of young people, he must expect at times to make sacrifices and to be inconvenienced.

At Ridgecrest one summer a superintendent of a Young People's department told how she had been enlisted. When the pastor and general superintendent approached her first, she declined. Her reason was she had too much to do without assuming any additional responsibility. They came back later asking her to reconsider. But she could not see any way to free herself from her other duties so that she might become superintendent.

Sometime later she became desperately ill and was rushed to a hospital, where it was found she needed a blood transfusion. On Sunday a request for blood donors was made in the Young People's department. A large number of young people responded. Going to the hospital, they waited outside her room, offering their blood to save her life. Seeing such a large number who were ready to give their blood made a profound impression upon her.

When she recovered from her illness, she came to her pastor and superintendent and offered herself for the leadership of the department. The willingness of the young people to serve her made her realize that serving them was more important than some other things she was doing.

The one who understands the ambitions and desires of young people and devotes himself to helping them achieve their goals will have their devotion and support. This will bring the teacher greater satisfaction than having young people serve him.

VI. Loyal to All Organizations in the Church

The church has a family of organizations with each one filling a place no other one can fill as well. Although the young people's teacher majors upon Sunday school work, he should always seek to create interest in the Training Union and in the organizations for young people, such as the Young Woman's Auxiliary and the Young Men's Brotherhood.

Every worker with young people should seek to enlist them in all the educational opportunities provided for them by the church. The teacher will have a better Sunday school class if the members attend the meetings of the other organizations regularly. The additional learning opportunities will bring greater personal development to each one who will take advantage of them. The entire program of the church will be advanced if the teacher also attends the meetings of the other organizations and, as far as possible, holds offices in them. This will demonstrate his belief in their value.

VII. Co-operating with the Work of His Denomination

Every teacher of young people should be proud of his Baptist heritage and lead the young people of his class to have a genuine regard for it also. This goal may be achieved in many ways but best of all by leading them to participate in activities with other Baptists.

Attending meetings conducted for the Baptists of an association is one of the finest ways of establishing wider denominational understanding and loyalty. Youth rallies, camps, the associational Sunday school organization, and other meetings will prove valuable to young people. More opportunities for fellowship and service exist now on the associational level than ever before. Every teacher should encourage young people to attend these meetings.

Young people may be led to work in the mission stations of the church and in Vacation Bible schools in their association. There are institutions where they may go with their teachers to conduct religious services. They should be encouraged to support associational missions by their contributions through the church budget.

The conventions, assemblies, and conferences conducted in many states afford young people excellent opportunities for wider denominational contacts.

Aside from the features of fellowship and contacts with denominational leaders is the added opportunity of discovering that one is a part of a great program in which hundreds of young people are interested. Young people from the smaller churches especially will be inspired by their contacts with larger numbers of young people in such an atmosphere.

The teacher should furnish information to the members of his class regarding the mission opportunities in his state.

He should acquaint those who plan to attend a college or university with the opportunities for training offered by the Baptist school or schools of his state. Young women who plan to become nurses should be informed regarding Baptist hospitals which offer this training.

Any opportunities for summer fieldwork should be understood, and these opportunities should be presented to young people interested in this program.

Southern Baptists maintain two assemblies for the instruction and inspiration of their constituency. The older of the two is located at Ridgecrest, North Carolina. The second one is located at Glorieta, New Mexico. Identical programs are offered at these assemblies each summer.

Of special significance to young people's teachers are the Sunday School Weeks. Programs each day provide for Bible study, inspirational messages, conferences on successful work with young people, and fellowship with others who teach this age group. Conferences for young people who attend are conducted also.

Of added interest to young people are the Training Union, Student Union, and Young Woman's Auxiliary Weeks. Many churches have found that money spent in making it possible for young people and their workers to attend one of these assemblies is one of their finest investments.

Those of experience and skill take part on the programs. The fellowship of young people from the various states of the Southern Baptist Convention enlarges their vision of service.

It is important also for the teacher to know the opportunities for church-related vocations which are open to young people in the Southern Baptist Convention. The demand for home and foreign missionaries is very great. Information regarding the types of workers which are needed and the requirements to be met may be secured from the Home Mission Board and the Foreign Mission Board.

Fieldworkers are needed in the various states for Sunday school, Vacation Bible school, Training Union, Woman's Missionary Union, and Brotherhood work.

Teachers are needed in denominational schools. Editors and writers are required for the denominational press. Writers are needed for editorial service. Administrators are in demand for denominational institutions.

In the local churches, in addition to the pastors, there is a great demand for ministers of religious education; ministers of music; directors of elementary and youth work; educational, financial, and other secretaries; and additional workers.

It is important for the young people's teacher to be acquainted with the opportunities for training offered by Baptist colleges and by the six Southern Baptist Seminaries. All of this information will prove helpful in properly relating the Young People of his class to the total work of his denomination.

VIII. Realizing the Cause Is Greater Than He Is

There will be times of crisis in the experience of every Christian worker. Unkind words, unjust criticism, and unfair indictments are to be expected. Each person must evaluate any criticism he receives and, if it is true, profit from it. But to let such things create issues which result in sharp personality clashes, bickerings, strife, and breach of fellowship in the church is a hindrance to the work of Christ in the community. Rather than permit such a situation to develop, it would be better for the teacher to give up his work quietly and accept some other place of service in the church.

The Bible abounds in counsel regarding one's relations with others. A teacher should read frequently Romans 12; 1 Corinthians 13; and Matthew 18:15-17. He will find that mastering himself is the greatest problem he will face. If he is willing to put loyalty to Christ and service to others above himself, the results of his work will never be in doubt.

IX. Profiting from These Relationships

Teaching is one of the most rewarding experiences one may have. To stay in touch with the rising tide of youth is a privilege indeed. Working with young people makes it possible for the teacher to have a part in guiding growing life at a time of great receptivity and impressionability. Often confidence and encouragement expressed at this time will be more meaningful than at any other period in life.

Teaching affords opportunities for the teacher to mature and develop. One's knowledge of the Bible is enlarged. He learns much of human nature and the varied problems of life. He develops understanding and sympathy. Success in the field of teaching may establish confidence for efforts in other fields. Sharing one's knowledge, experience, and love with others gives greater meaning to life.

The talents the teacher possesses increase in effectiveness through use. One's intellect becomes keener through study and stimulating experiences in the classroom. One's social graces are cultivated in contacts with members and fellow workers in the Sunday school. In presenting the most attractive appeal possible for attendance and enlistment, the teacher becomes more alert and interesting. Learning to express himself before his class, to pray in public, and to give young people the leadership they need, will result in the growth of one's spiritual life.

One learns to teach by teaching. In learning to teach, the teacher himself is taught. One of the greatest rewards comes from the realization that one is working with Christ in a task that he wants done. As the teacher renders his service in the name of Christ, he depends upon his Master for the unusual strength needed for this responsibility. He finds Christ's presence becomes more real to him, even as the Master promised. It is this realization of contact with Christ which strengthens the faith and spiritual power of every teacher.

FOR FURTHER STUDY

1. Does your Sunday school have a weekly officers and teachers meeting? If so, what is your percentage of attendance? Are you satisfied with it?
2. How many training opportunities has your church had during the past year? Have you taken advantage of them? Toward which diploma in the Church Study Course are you now working?
3. Is your church represented in associational, state, and Southern Baptist Convention meetings? What can you do to make this representation possible? to increase it?
4. "Count your many blessings" as a teacher of young people. Pray for a growing leadership life.

SUGGESTIONS FOR THE TEACHER

WHO WILL LEAD IN THE STUDY OF THIS BOOK

Your teaching of this book should demonstrate principles which the book sets forth. In preparation, consider what you will do to learn of the interests, experience, abilities, and needs of those who will be in your study class. Write out your aim, based on (1) the known and anticipated needs of the members of the study group and (2) on the contents of this book.

For each session of the class time consider (1) how to develop an atmosphere conducive to learning, (2) how to arouse and utilize the sense of need on the part of members of the study class, (3) how to secure participation, and (4) how to lead members to put into practice in their teaching the principles which have been brought out in the class sessions.

Study the main heads on the chapter outlines for ideas for thought questions which will promote discussion and participation. As the group brings out points, list them on the chalkboard. Then lead the class to refer to the chapter outline or the author's discussion for further points.

Plan to involve your members in learning activities. The points under "For Further Study" at the end of each chapter will give you suggestions. Many of these aim at increasing a sense of need and leading members to definite plans for improvement.

Encourage the class members to exchange ideas about how to carry out the principles and methods discovered in the study of the chapter.

Use audio-visual aids. The filmstrips in the "Teacher Improvement Series" can be used effectively with the chapters indicated: *The Christian Teacher* (chaps. 1, 2, or 8), *Selecting Aims* (chap. 4), *Choosing Methods* (chap. 5), *Planning a Lesson* (chap. 6), *Testing Results* (chap. 8).

The motion pictures *Preparing to Teach* (15 min.) and *Teaching the Word* (15 min.) will also prove very effective. A utilization guide may be requested when the film is ordered from the Baptist Book Store.

As a climax to the whole study you may show the motion picture *The Great Challenge* (30 min.).

In addition to, or instead of, the activities listed under "For

Further Study" you may wish to lead the study group to do some of the following:

Chapter 1.—Build a self-rating chart for a teacher of young people. In private, each worker may score himself now, lay away the chart, then score himself again at the end of six months or a year.

Chapter 3.—Share ideas of how Sunday school teachers may gain the information they need about their class members.

Chapter 4.—Consider the aims stated for the current quarter as a whole and for groups of lessons and each lesson. Compare these aims with the basic aims stated on pages 55–60 to discover which of the basic aims will find some achievement during this quarter. (For this study you will need the Preview Study which appears in *The Young People's Teacher.* The preview for any given quarter appears in the third month of the preceding quarter. If you are in the last month of the quarter, you may wish to use the preview study for the next quarter's lesson.)

Chapter 5.—Use the leaflet "What Methods Shall I Use When I Teach?" as supplementary material. (Available from your state Sunday school secretary or from the Sunday School Department, Baptist Sunday School Board, Nashville, Tennessee 37203.)

Chapters 6 and 7.—Following the study of chapter 6, write out a teaching plan for next Sunday's lesson. As chapter 7 is studied, class members should share their proposed plans for (1) creating a good atmosphere for learning, (2) securing attention and interest, (3) getting participation, (4) leading the class to worthwhile conclusions, and (5) stimulating further learning.

Chapter 9.—Use a nine-member panel to present the nine points covered in this chapter. Follow with questions and testimonies from the group.

FOR REVIEW AND WRITTEN WORK

Chapter 1

1. Why is the teacher's place a position of honor and trust?
2. Give four necessary qualifications of a teacher of young people. How would you rate yourself regarding these: below average, average, or above average?
3. Why is a teacher's enthusiasm so important?

Chapter 2

4. What are four unsatisfactory concepts of teaching? Which of these seems to be the most generally accepted?
5. Is it correct to refer to teaching as an art? Give reasons for your answer.
6. What kinds of participation is the teacher attempting to secure during the teaching process?
7. When has a teacher taught?

Chapter 3

8. What factors are responsible for the difference in young people?
9. State some areas of their lives in which young people are making significant adjustments.
10. Why and how should a teacher take the initiative in enlisting members.
11. What is meant by "remaining objective" in evaluation?

Chapter 4

12. Indicate three values in having aims for teaching.
13. What are the two types of aims? Indicate the difference in them.
14. What should guide the teacher in selecting aims for teaching?
15. Suggest some values of frequent discussion of aims at the weekly officers and teachers' meeting.

Chapter 5

16. Do you consider the method of teaching important? Give reasons for your manner.
17. What factors guide a teacher in selecting a method of teaching. Which method do you use the most? Why?

Chapter 6

18. List the study habits discussed in this chapter. How many of these have you already formed? What will you do about the others?
19. Name the sources of lesson helps mentioned by the author. Check those which are available to you.
20. What areas of experience are involved in a teacher's preparation?
21. Cite nine steps in the process of preparing a lesson plan.

Chapter 7

22. List several things a teacher can do to secure good surroundings in which to teach?
23. What should take place during the brief portion of the class period when the president is in charge?
24. Cite three principles to follow in securing attention and interest.
25. Name some ways in which a teacher may encourage participation by class members.
26. Suggest a helpful way to lead class members to arrive at some satisfactory conclusions as a result of a lesson.

Chapter 8

27. Why is it important for a teacher to evaluate his teaching?
28. Look over the list of questions under the heading, "Teaching Succeeds as the Teacher Grows." How would you rate yourself on these: below average, average, above average?

Chapter 9

29. What are some significant areas of interpersonal relationships for the teacher?
30. Should a teacher be concerned about what others think? Why?
31. Why is it important for a teacher to be in harmony with the leadership of the church?